Stories *from* Before

Stories *from* Before

The New Voices
of Immigrants in St. Louis

Selected and Edited by

Janet Morey and **Gail Schafers**

Photography by Janet and Art Morey

Missouri Historical Society Press
St. Louis

To Pepe with our deep thanks

© 2007 by the Missouri Historical Society Press
All rights reserved

Designed by Madonna Gauding

Library of Congress Cataloging-in-Publication Data

Stories from before : the new voices of immigrants in St. Louis / selected and edited by Janet Morey and Gail Schafers.
p. cm.
Summary: "In more than forty collected stories, immigrants living in St. Louis write compelling accounts of their earlier lives"--Provided by publisher.
Rev. ed. of: Old stories in a new land / [selected and edited by] Janet Morey. 2005.
ISBN 978-1-883982-62-1 (hardcover : alk. paper)
1. Saint Louis (Mo.)--Ethnic relations--Anecdotes. 2. Immigrants--Missouri--Saint Louis--Biography--Anecdotes. 3. Ethnology--Missouri--Saint Louis--Anecdotes. 4. Saint Louis (Mo.)--Biography--Anecdotes. 5. English language--Study and teaching--Foreign speakers--Anecdotes. I. Morey, Janet. II. Schafers, Gail. III. Old stories in a new land.
F474.S29A265 2007
920.0086'91209778'66--dc22
[B]
2007041508

Printed and bound by Thomson-Shore, Inc.
11 10 09 08 07 1 2 3 4 5

Contents

Foreword

When I was quite young, I inherited a coloring book from my big sister, Anne. It was called, I remember, *Children of Other Lands*. Anne had colored most of the pages, so this was more like a picture book for me. The pictures were simple, just line drawings with little detail; but Anne was a careful and imaginative colorist, and the children in their brightly crayoned native costumes kept me entertained for many an hour.

As I try to recall how the little-boy me viewed those faraway children, it does seem that they were as completely strange and foreign as the 1950s superheroes in my comic books, no one I would ever meet or visit or certainly understand. Although nothing seems totally impossible to a six-year-old, the distance from my boyhood home in Michigan's Upper Peninsula to, say, Japan or Argentina made a trip to any of those "other lands" as remote as a visit to the outer rings of Saturn.

Of course, the world and even the universe have gotten smaller, and not without some humility I know that my perspective has expanded. I am fortunate to count among my close acquaintances a number of people from "other lands," and many from different cultures and traditions, races, and religions. But I have had little opportunity to immerse myself in a culture other than my own, and so I rely on an ancient method of understanding people different from me: I listen to their stories.

This volume contains within its pages a charming variety of new voices "from other lands," even though they were written right here in St. Louis. These people are your neighbors, the folks in front of you in the grocery store or in the adjacent lane on the highway. The younger students might be the kids at the local movie house or at the mall. But their stories help us to see the vast differences our region embraces and the common ground of the human experience. Reading them opens a new path to community that is an immediate necessity to a more peaceful world and a more sustainable future.

Robert R. Archibald, Ph.D.
President, Missouri Historical Society

Introduction

At the start of every school term, international students enter educational institutions all across the St. Louis area, weighed down by stuffed backpacks, textbooks, notebooks—and uncertainty. Many do not speak or understand English readily, much less write in their second language. Usually hesitant, most appear shy and tentative as they settle a bit uncomfortably into their desks.

At this point, these students remain unaware that before long, they will discover a precious shared commodity. Each of them embraces a store of mental keepsakes as real and as uniquely theirs as the objects they lovingly place into suitcases prior to leaving their countries. As the school year progresses, writing teachers will encourage them to unpack these memories, carefully sort through them, and organize them. Assignments to call back childhood experiences invariably elicit the most touching responses. Closest to the heart, they resonate with the innocence of youth.

"Let your ideas pour onto that paper!" we teachers instruct. But it's not that easy. Students labor as they dust off these "memories from before." They think hard to recall details. They toil to choose just the right words. Later, they tighten their writing and finally, they polish it, until it gleams to their satisfaction. "Writing is all about feelings," we tell them, and they believe us when this process evokes joy, sadness, heartbreak, triumph. A small child recalls (and misses) the White Moon Festival in Mongolia. A young Bosnian remembers nearly drowning in the Adriatic Sea before she and her friend hailed a fishing boat. Another writes about a cold winter in Korea, when she helped her mother push a milk cart through the streets to make deliveries.

Students thrill to discover their writing voices, and we teachers pause to appreciate the enormous privilege of working with these people. "Surely, these stories must be shared," we comment to each other. The tales, collected over the past eight years or so and appearing here in *Stories from Before: The New Voices of Immigrants in St. Louis*, emanate from students aged eleven through eighty-five, from elementary school through graduate programs.

We, the compilers, invite you to find a quiet spot, study and enjoy the black and white portraits of these writers, and then delve into the compelling accounts of their earlier lives.

Please Note: We asked each of our adult contributors to include a brief autobiography. As for the elementary school children, we omitted autobiographies, as we felt this was too much to ask.

Xuemin "Charles" Kou

In 1963, I was born in a small village, Koujiacun, Shaanxi State, in the middle of China. My Chinese name is Kou Xuemin; Kou is my family name, and Xuemin is my given name. During my first years, China's economy was very poor. Most people had nothing to eat, and some people died from starvation. My home was also short of grain and food, so that my body was weak then.

I finished my primary school in my village. But I did not get anything from the school because the educational system was in disorder from the government. The students did not need to study. They just needed to work on their farms every day, the government said. That was bad.

In 1979, I went to a small town fifteen miles from my village to start high school. The town was in the center of our county. The big building there excited me because I had never seen it before.

In 1983, after finishing high school, I went to Shaanxi Financial College to major in foreign trade (international business). In 1985, I was dispatched by this school to study in Xiamen University, located in Fujian State, because my major was better there than at other universities. Xiamen City is a beautiful coastal city. I still remember the tall flowering trees and my dormitory in a red building.

The government gave me a good job when I graduated from the university in 1987. (In those times, all graduates had jobs assigned by the government, and we did not need to find work for ourselves. However, now all graduates must find their own work; the government no longer provides jobs.) I was assigned to a state-owned company that worked in international business. My job was to seek for products to export from

our region to our headquarters. Then the products could be exported to other countries.

I had this position for four years, and later I found a new job in a coastal city in southern China. I worked there until I came to America in 2001. Now I am studying English at Fontbonne University in St. Louis, Missouri, and am continuing my major there. I will return to China after I get a degree. I think success depends on individual struggle, and we get good repayment so long as we like to pay out.

⅔ ⅔ ⅔

Father—Bicycle—Snow

In spite of wherever I am today, how can I forget that memorable sight— my father taking me to the hospital on an old, shabby bicycle through thick snow on a muddy countryside road in the middle of China during a cold winter. . . .

It happened in my father's hometown the very chill winter of 1972. I was eight years old and in Grade 2 then. One day after school, I invited some of my classmates to play a game with me in the big yard of our house. It was a children's game, but it is still very funny and interesting even today. All of us boys were friendly—madly fighting, hiding from each other, and shooting each other with wooden guns. We were all so happy at that time that I forgot about the dry well in the yard. Unfortunately, I did not pay attention and fell down into that well which was about twenty feet deep. I cried from the bottom of the well and felt horrible because I saw just the sky looking like a small dish above me when I lifted my head up. My confused playmates' voices were almost inaudible.

About a half-hour passed. My father came from our farmland after one of my friends called him. (I think my mother was far away in another village at that time.) My father asked two or three neighbors to help him without delay. He bundled himself with a long rope and went down

3

along the wall of the well to the bottom quickly. When I saw my father, I cried more. My tears were so many and could not stop. He wrapped me with another rope and let the men who were standing on the ground draw the rope. I was lifted up at last. My leg was broken. It hurt me very much, and I cried all night. I could even touch some broken bones of my leg under my skin. My father could not sleep, and he used some cloth belt to wrap my leg tightly.

The next morning, it was snowing heavily, and there were about five inches of packed snow on the ground. The land, houses, and trees were all pure white. The snow continued. . . . My father wanted to take me by bicycle to go to the hospital that was ten miles away from our house. We wore warm coats and brought some dry steamed buns with us to eat on the way. At about 10 a.m., we started out in hard snow. On the white and bending road, there was not any bicycle or person, only my father and I. Because of the bad weather, my father, who wore a thick cotton cap and an old woolen muffler, could not ride the bicycle; he could only push it on the snowy road. The bicycle wheels were pasted with mud and snow and ice. We almost could not see. That was so hard and made my father tired, every time he moved even one step. I could not do anything for him, but only sat on the bicycle. My father, huffing and puffing, pushed the bicycle step by step. Snowflakes covered his cap and coat; he looked like a snowman.

I clearly remember that when we got to the hospital, it was dark. My father was so exhausted that he could not stand as he talked to the doctors. One doctor told my father that if he had not gotten me to the hospital then, maybe my leg would have lost normal ability forever.

Even though it was more than thirty years ago, how can I forget the sight of my kind and peaceful father taking me by bicycle and walking along the snowy road slowly? Today I often make phone calls to my father. When we mention those old things, my father and I are still moved, and my tears come down.

Xuemin "Charles" Kou, China
Fontbonne University MBA Program

Sandrine Jallon

I was born July 16, 1967, near Saint-Etienne, a big French urban center known for its industries, its famous Weiss chocolate, and its football team (soccer in the United States), the "Greens." I grew up fifteen miles away from the city, surrounded by woods in a "strange house"—as qualified at that time by people—designed by my father, Andre, an architect. My mother, Danielle, took care of my brother, Fabien, and me.

Interested in languages, I studied English, German, and Russian, as well as philosophy. I developed a passion for German and for Germany, where my two best friends are now living. After receiving my high school diploma, I studied communications, specializing in government agencies. I began to work as a communications assistant during my last year of school in a town close to Lyon. The political team, as well as the administration, was so kind that I had the feeling I was protected. We were all taking care of each other, developing our knowledge like children in their families.

After three years, I took more responsibility in the service. In 1994, I was offered the position of communications director in Saint-Etienne. The challenge was attractive, and the four years I spent there flew like minutes. I learned how to manage teams of people and large amounts of money, as well as how to fight like a wolf to be heard—just because I was a young woman.

In 1998, my partner was offered a promotion to Belgium by his American company, and I decided to go with him. We spent two years in Brussels—in the rain—before moving to St. Louis, where we enjoy the color of the sky every day! The same year, in August, we got married. He

is still working for that company, and we are both students again. My husband will soon earn an MBA from Washington University, and I will get an MA in communications from Lindenwood University.

꩜ ꩜ ꩜

"Please, Don't Touch!"

Have you ever heard or seen this order? Surely, yes. As far back as I remember, I have heard this little order said with a kind or a frightening voice: as a child while my mother was bringing out of the oven her gold-brown apple-cinnamon tart, and I wanted to take a piece of it before it became cold, and as an adult while I have been visiting the sculpture section of art museums.

Touching things is often a real pleasure. Sometimes, you just need to close your eyes and move your hands. You make your fingers the longest you can, you put your palm as flat as possible, and you are ready to feel: feel the soft, smooth skin of your lover, the roughness of an old tree trunk, the magic force of stones. But sometimes, you have to imagine the feeling because the only way you can touch is doing it with your eyes when touching is forbidden. Unfortunately, but understandably, it's the case in museums.

Once, and I am not proud of it, I put my left hand on the head of a sphinx. I was at the Louvre, walking in another world, ancient Egypt. Nobody saw me, and I wasn't punished for one of the strongest moments of my life. The stone was cold like my grandfather's gravestone and lightly bumpy like an apricot crumble. But that's not the important thing. Touching this four-thousand-year-old sculpture made me different. I realized, at that moment, the power of touch. It was like a painless hit. At that precise moment, I was able to *see* with my hand. It made my imagination work. I was not anymore in a museum. I was inside a pyramid, climbing up stairs, trying to figure out which place would be the best one for "my sphinx"!

Now, I often use my sense of touch in everyday life, when I am buying fruits or furniture for the house—which are not exactly the same—when I am cooking or gardening, especially when I have to make the earth as light as sand. It is like pressing a button, and my imagination is on. In my dreams, I am a sculptor. I have a gallery where people don't come to buy. It's written everywhere: please, touch!

Sandrine Jallon, France
Parkway AEL Program
Lindenwood University Graduate Program

Quianaca J. Wesseh

My name is Quianaca J. Wesseh. I was born in the year 1976, on June 10, in Bong County, Liberia, West Africa. My mother's name was Mary Nyemah, and my father's name was Brown W. Wesseh. My parents have seven living children. I am a high school graduate and have a proficiency certificate in house plumbing, as well as a certificate in African gospel music.

During the Liberian Civil War, my father was killed. Later I went to Côte d'Ivoire (the Ivory Coast) as a Liberian refugee, and I applied to the United Nations High Commission for Refugees (UNHCR) for resettlement. The UNHCR accepted my application.

I entered the United States through an agency called the International Organization for Migration (IOM). People from the International Institute in St. Louis met me at the airport and helped me find my baggage. They also found me a job and a place to sleep. When I arrived in St. Louis, it was wintertime. I was surprised to see no leaves on the trees. I thought that all the trees everywhere had died!

Now, I am living in my own apartment, working and studying full time, and enjoying my church friends.

The Witch Doctor's "Son"

In one of the poor countries of Africa, Liberia, I was told to go to the interior to live with my uncle. My uncle had never had a child, and since my parents had many children, he had come to our home and had chosen me. He wanted to raise me as his son. This custom was not unusual in the interior.

My uncle was the chief witch doctor and leader of the witchcraft society in Liberia. The year was 1985, and I was nine years old.

I was not happy living in the interior because there was no school and only witchcraft. My uncle told me to work with him, serving him whenever he was performing his craft. The people in the town called me the son of the witch doctor. This always made me mad.

One day I thought it wise to escape from Jackarken, my uncle's town. I wanted to continue my schooling. I found a road to the city, and soon I entered a small village of only two houses, where I rested for two days. My leaving Jackarken for two days brought a serious concern to the strong men of the town. They searched for me and found me in the little village. The man who had hosted me was beaten almost to death, and the village was burned. I was taken back to Jackarken. I continued to serve my uncle.

After two months, my uncle took sick and died suddenly. One week later, all the men and women of Jackarken dressed in sack clothes, preparing to dance. As the "son" of the witch doctor, I was dressed by the wizard. The right side of my body was painted with red, the left side with black. The Jackarkens were automatically preparing me to be installed as chief witch doctor of the town. I didn't know what was going on. There was a big black medicine pot that couldn't be broken. The pot also could not touch the ground. After the people danced and mourned for my uncle for about two hours, everyone sat down. I was told to stand in the middle of the town. The witch doctors brought the fearful-looking medicine pot to me, telling me to hold it and drink from it. I didn't know what was in it. While everyone was silently looking at me, I held the pot and reached up to God and said, "Father, you never made me to be a witch doctor. Please take control right now."

I dropped the medicine pot on the ground, and it split into pieces. Everybody in the town scattered with fear. In the meantime, I ran to the bush, and the witch doctors ran after me. They never saw me. I hid in the bush for half a day. I was tired, and I slept. A hunter passed by, saw me, and woke me up, asking what I was doing in the bush, and what had happened. I explained my reason for being there. I told him that I wanted to go to the city and continue my education. The hunter took me to the city, and I lived with one of his brothers. There I stayed and finished my education.

Here I am today in the city of St. Louis with the guidance and the blessing of almighty God.

Quianaca J. Wesseh, Liberia
International Institute

Celia Maria Flexa

The second child of three (two girls and a boy), I was born in Brazil on December 23, 1949. I grew up in a small city, Itu, where I had my education until I reached college. I taught math, science, history, and Portuguese at a basic school. I had a great professional experience.

In 1973 I married Roberto Flexa, and we moved to São Paulo City. We have three daughters who still live in Brazil. I don't have grandchildren yet, but I would love to.

Because of my husband's job, we moved to Mexico City in 1997 and to St. Louis in 1999. I like living here. The people are friendly and very polite. But I miss my family and country so much. We will eventually go back to Brazil.

The Train Trip

One of the most pleasant memories that I have from my childhood is the trip that we—my father, my sister, and I—took to visit my grandparents.

I was around four or five years old, and my sister was one year older than I was. To reach my grandparents' town, Amparo, we took the train in a small town, Valinhos, to a bigger town, Campinas, to take another train pushed by a steam locomotive. This trip, which takes fifty minutes by car now, took three hours at that time. It was wonderful to hear the

locomotive making me fall asleep with its soft *choo-choo* and then suddenly waking me with its whistle before each curve or tunnel.

I still can see the small pieces of bright red embers coming through the train window and my dad closing it quickly so our clothes would not burn. And I remember that when part of the trip had finished, a man wearing a uniform and a cap came by, piercing all the passengers' tickets and informing us of the next city we would stop at.

How great it was when we arrived at my grandparents', and they were waiting for us in their warm house with a big table full of food! Especially I remember the delicious bread pudding that only my grandma knew how to make—or maybe it was the flavor of a grandmother's love that only a child can taste.

Celia Maria Flexa, Brazil
Parkway AEL Program

Mikako Nishi

I was born on a small tropical island that is located in the southern part of Japan. Its name is Kikai Island. I lived there until I graduated from high school. I like my hometown because it is beautiful, calm, and warm. My parents are still living there.

My family includes my parents, two brothers, and me. When I was a child, I often fought with my brothers. My parents always told me that I had to help my mother because I was a girl. Therefore, at that time, I didn't like my brothers very much. But now, I like them so much, and they are important to me. My brothers help me now; I respect my parents and my brothers.

After I graduated from high school, I moved to Tokyo, the capital of Japan. I went to a special school for training as a medical secretary for two years. After that, I worked at a hospital as a receptionist for eight years. I enjoyed my job because I like to talk to people and to help people.

Now I am in the United States to study English because my boyfriend is here, and I want to speak English well. I enjoy studying English and living in St. Louis. It is a beautiful city, everybody is kind to me, and I have made many American friends and other friends from different countries. Since I came here, I have learned not only English, but I have learned about different cultures and different viewpoints.

I have been in St. Louis for a year and three months, but I am thinking I will go back to Japan this summer. I know that I still need to study English, but I miss my country, my family, and my job. I will continue to study English in Japan. Then, I hope to travel to many countries to visit the friends I met here in St. Louis. I really like America. My American

life has been a good experience for me. And the friends whom I have met here have become my treasures.

⁊ ⁊ ⁊

The Big Hand of My Father

When I was a child, my parents sometimes scolded me because I didn't always obey my parents. Actually I don't remember specific times when they scolded me, and why they scolded me, because always it was my fault. But I just remember once when my father slapped my face strongly.

One day, when I was in third or fourth grade, I played outside until evening with my two friends. And then my one friend and I took the other friend, who lived a little far from our place, home. So I got home after the sun had set.

When I got home, my father was very angry, and he didn't allow me to go inside the house because I had gotten home late. He asked me why I got home late. At the time I didn't tell the truth because I didn't understand why my father was so angry. I kept silent. After that, my father slapped my face strongly once. I was surprised by that and I, with tears of vexation, was also getting angry because I didn't know why I was slapped by my father. I still kept silent in my stubbornness because I thought that I had just taken my friend home! It was not my fault! After that, he slapped me again. And he went inside the house without me.

After a few hours, my father came over to me, and he asked me again why I had gotten home late. Finally I told him everything while I cried. He asked me why I had not said that earlier, but I would say only, "I'm sorry."

I don't know if my father still remembers that he slapped me, but now he sometimes says, "Mikako was the most stubborn of my children." Moreover, I cannot forget that my father slapped my face, and that my whole face hurt, even though he slapped only my left cheek.

Mikako Nishi, Japan
Fontbonne University

18

Milan Horacek

My name is Milan Horacek, and I come from a small country in the middle of Europe called the Czech Republic. I was born as the only child of my parents in a small town close to the Polish border. It is a nice part of the country with high mountains and lots of woods, with places to hike, ride, bike, and enjoy the many wonders of nature. People who like the outdoors appreciate this area a lot. My parents were definitely those people. We often went for long trips or bike rides and camping. I feel fortunate to have grown up in such a wonderful place and to have such nice parents who wanted to spend so much time with me.

After nine years of basic school, which is how the school system works in my country, I went to high school to study artistic carpentry. I graduated with honors but decided not to pursue a career in this field. It was just not in me to settle down like most of my friends. I had always dreamed about going to faraway places, but I realized that dreaming was not enough. I also needed to do something about my dreams. I worked for a short time for my dad who is a textile designer, and then I left for England. I spent a few truly memorable years there, picking up English as I went along—through a number of embarrassing situations and through hours over books, trying to figure out the meaning of what I was reading. After experiencing life in England, I came back home, but I did not stay long.

Next I went to Australia. My life abroad was not always easy. I went through jobs I would not be willing to do back home, but I did that just to be able to save money for traveling at the end of staying there. In my opinion it was more than worth it. It was an incredible feeling to be "on the road," everything I needed in my backpack, the blue sky above

me, and unknown adventures ahead of me. Who can ever describe how it feels to fall asleep in the desert under the open sky, with myriads of stars shining above hundreds of miles of civilization? I was listening to the sounds of the night and thinking, trying to figure out who I was and where I was heading in life.

When I returned home, I did not stay for very long again but decided to come here to America. I have visited nice places in the world, but I did not have anybody to share them with. I felt I was missing something. Then I met the sweetest girl, my love, and now, my wonderful wife. She likes the same things as I do. It feels so nice to share and experience everything with her now. Here in America I have found not only nature's wonders and continuing adventurous experiences, but also a second home and the love of my life.

Winnetou, Old Shatterhand, and Me

I have many childhood memories. Some of them contain "big adventures," others just small everyday events, not important in any way, but still somehow entrapped in my mind. However, to think about the one thing that had a big influence on me through my whole childhood and formed me into the way I am today is probably my love for reading.

I liked reading even when I could not read yet. I remember the times in the morning when my dad left for work that I crept into my mom's bed, and she read to me. At first she read the books which were usual for small children, but later she shared even the books for children much older than I was. For example, she read the Tarzan book. I would just listen with an open mouth about his adventures as lord of the jungle. Later I couldn't comprehend when my mom was surprised how much I loved climbing trees!

When I got older and could read on my own, I read whatever I could get my hands on. The writer of my childhood was Karl May, the German author, who wrote books about Winnetou, the Apache chief, and his white "blood brother," Old Shatterhand. They were roaming together around the Wild West, fighting the bad people among the white people as well as among the Indians and helping everybody who needed it. Today I know that Karl May's books were fiction, not reflecting reality, but thanks to his books I developed an affection for everything that was connected with the American West and Indians. The life of the Indians seemed to be so adventurous and romantic to me. I dreamed about what it would be like to live back then in an Indian tepee, hunting buffalos, and I felt so sorry for myself that I was not born in those exciting times.

Because I was always very sensitive, everything somehow affected me more than other children my age. I read so much that my parents started to worry about me. My dad did not want me to read those books anymore, but I liked them so much that I could not stop. I was reading at night under the pillow with a torch. I also had a secret hideout up in the beech tree in our garden. I don't remember how many books I read there. That was a place where I felt very special overlooking our town, reading and dreaming about all the places I wanted to go. My favorite spot was at the very top of the tree, where the branches were still strong enough to support me and where the view from the tree was the best, not overshadowed by other branches. There I could feel like Tarzan or like an Indian looking down to the far sides of the town and across to the horizon.

Some of the best memories I have of this place happened during the early spring. The leaves were fresh green, everything had started blossoming, and even the air smelled different. There was something about that spring breeze that is difficult to describe even today. To me it seemed like it was full of newness and promise. I remember me, sitting up in my tree, smelling that mysterious spring and listening to the distant whistle of locomotives and the sound of trains going far away. At that time I longed to go with one of those trains and experience the adventures that I was reading about. Now, after the years, I am sure that through my child's eyes, everything looked more fascinating than I would see it today, but I still liked it a lot.

My "Indian fever," as my parents called it, eventually cooled off somewhat, but the feeling to go somewhere far away and see what was behind the far horizon, was still in me. My dreams came partly true, and I was able to travel. Now when I am here in America, it is a nice feeling to walk the places I was always reading about and learn more about their history. Being in America is part of my childhood dream—which came true. I am grateful for that!

Milan Horacek, Czech Republic
St. Louis Community College

Hye Kyong Park

I was born in Jeon Buk, Korea, which is south of Seoul. My family immigrated to Los Angeles, California, when I was eleven years old. So many things happened to me after I left Korea. Thinking back, I remember most significantly wondering how I could not get adjusted to America. Before I came, I had dreamed that I was going to be walking on golden roads, but the reality was totally shocking.

Because of the language barrier, I had no close friends for a long time, and I did not do well in school. Most of all, I had the hardest time adjusting to American food. I could not even eat half of the hamburger that everybody liked because it was too greasy. Naturally, I longed for my country and was fortunate enough to go back home to Korea from time to time.

Then, early in 1990, I declared my independence from my family. I was only twenty years old. (It is not common for a Korean woman to be separated from her family before her marriage.) I met many new people and was fully enjoying the freedom that I earned for the first time. During that time I met my best friend, Min Kyong, who is still my best friend. Those have been the climax years of my life so far.

Now I live in St. Louis with my sister and her family. They have two sons, Justin and Brandon, whom I adore dearly. I work full time at a beauty supply store. I don't know which direction God will lead me from here, but I am sure that He will lead me to the green pasture that He has planned for me. My wish for the near future is to meet a soul mate and settle down once and for all, in the United States of America.

The Unwanted Gift

My childhood memories are full of scars and tears. When I was growing up, our family had to move many times. I was eleven years old when my family moved to Los Angeles, California, from South Korea. As soon as we got to the United States, my Aunt Heidi enrolled me in the Beverly Hills Elementary School. I did not speak any English or understand it, so naturally I did not want to go. But the choice was not given to me.

I remember my first days of school. There were no blacks or Asians in any of my classes. In fact, I was probably the only Asian in the whole Beverly Hills Elementary School. I know many teachers tried to help me in many ways so I could fit in comfortably, but it was the most confusing time of my life. During lunch times, many students came to my classroom to see me because I was different from them. They treated me like a monkey in a cage; everybody stared at me because I looked different. They were talking to me and asking many questions, but I did not understand at all. It took me a couple of days to figure out that they were only making fun of me. Since they could not communicate with me, they started making gestures, such as making slant eyes with their hands. And they pointed fingers at me. They hurt my feelings too much for me to want to go back to school every day. I crossed my fingers and prayed every night for Friday to come faster.

But there was one boy who did not make fun of me and did not think it funny when everyone else was teasing me. His name was Michael, and he was my angel. He fought for me when I was weak, he guarded me from others' steps on my pride, and he comforted me when they were all over me, waiting to see whether I would shed the last drops of tears that I had been trying to save. He was my hero and my knight.

There was one incident that I will never forget. As always, Michael was protecting me from those obnoxious students, and I felt especially thankful for him that day. So I decided to give him a gift, the gift that I have enjoyed very much even up to now. I wrapped a dried squid, took it to school, and gave it to Michael. As soon as he opened the gift and saw what it was, he jumped out of his chair and ran away from me.

Michael did not come near me for a whole week. I was in agony and in great fear of losing my one and only hero at school. I begged Aunt Heidi to call Michael at home and find out what I did wrong, and why he was not coming near me. She did call Michael's mom, and they talked a long time. I made sure that my aunt told Michael's mom that the gift was sincere and a token of my appreciation for all his help and support during my most difficult time. From that point, we became the best of buddies, not to mention that he was the very first boy who kissed me on the cheek.

I learned many valuable lessons during those first few years living in America. But the most unforgettable lesson I learned was that *Americans do not like dried squid!*

Hye Kyong Park, Korea
Parkway AEL Program

Sina Sadridahaj

I was born in 1975 in Yazd, Iran. My father died in a car accident when I was three months old, so our mom had to take care of my two brothers and me.

Ever since the Islamic Revolution in 1977 in Iran, my religion, which is Baha'i, has not been very welcome, so as a Baha'i, I had to fight many challenges. I was young, and I had a lot of wishes to reach. I decided to leave my family, friends, and everything I had and move from Iran to the United States. It was very hard, but I did it.

I have a lot of memories from my old life, good and bad. I started a new life in the United States and met very good people to help me to get through it. To achieve my goals, I have to be educated, so I became a student of St. Louis Community College. I would like to be a computer engineer, no matter how long it will take or how hard it will be.

I never give up because I believe that life is in our hands, and we can take it wherever we want.

My Favorite Place

My room was not big and not small. There was a bed in the middle, a small green desk with leather chair that was placed near the window, and a beautiful rug on the floor. Also there was a big closet in the corner of it. That closet was my favorite place and my hiding place too.

It was a huge one with three shelves. I used the first two to put my clothes, shoes, and my school stuff. But the third one was very special to me. I hung a couple of my parents' pictures on the wall, and also there were all my favorite things, such as gifts that I got on my birthdays, some old money that was left from my grandmother, and some stamps.

I have a lot of memories from that closet. As a little child, it was a place where I would always feel safe and relaxed. I would always hide in there, and my mom could not find me for a couple of hours. One time I missed the school bus because of playing with other kids, and I had to walk all the way home. When I got home, I realized that my mom was so worried about me, and I went straight to my safe place, and I hid there for more hours! (Oh well, after a while, the first place my mom would check to find me was the closet, of course!)

You may wonder how I could hide there for hours? I had a candle which would light my closet just enough so that I could close the door and sit there forever. My mom would come and call me, but for some reason my voice would never come out to answer. Whenever I got mad at something I ran in the closet and kept thinking and thinking. I would think about my dreams, what I wanted to do when I grew up, what the world looked like. It was so funny; it was like I could not use my brain unless I was in the closet! I was so sensitive about everything, and that place would make me feel safe and secure and important.

I believe every person has a "closet." No matter what age or where in the world, everyone needs a place to be alone, a place to make herself or himself feel protected and relaxed. Some people go to churches, some go walking and listen to music, some go to a cemetery and pray, and some sit at their desk and think. Fortunately, I do not get in a closet anymore. But I will never forget my closet in my room.

Sina Sadridahaj, Iran
St. Louis Community College

Nicole "Nicky" Miezi Deprez

My name is Nicky Miezi Deprez. I was born in Kinshasa, Zaire. I lived in Virginia for two years and then in St. Louis for six years before my family and I moved to Florida. I'm sixteen years old, and I'm in the tenth grade at a private high school in St. Louis County.

Except when I am attending school, I live in Orlando, Florida, with my mother and two older brothers, Phil and Rich. I love to spend time with my family, travel, play basketball, and listen to music. I especially love to read any and all books that I can find.

I'm proud and grateful to be able to share my story with everyone who gets to read this book.

From Zaire to America

The year 1992 marked an extreme time in the history of Zaire. My family and I were caught in the middle of a chilling civil war. I was around four, my brother Richard was eleven, and my brother Phil was thirteen. We stayed in our house constantly, too scared to go out. We could smell the fear in the air. Gunshots became a continual sound every day and every night: African against African, soldiers in the street killing each other and even shooting townspeople mercilessly.

I remember that my brothers and their friends would sit on the wall surrounding our house to listen to the bullets whiz through the air. Everything in our city, Kinshasa, was either destroyed or taken over by

guerilla warriors: stores, houses, parks, hotels, schools. Soon we were forced to escape from our house because it was to be seized. Danger increased daily.

My mother, my brothers, and I ended up hiding in an abandoned building with another family who were close friends. Aware of the warfare, my dad had left us in Kinshasa a couple of months earlier, to survive on our own. He had never really planned on helping us out of the country. As a government official for USAID, he traveled away from home for long periods of time. My parents' relationship was on the rocks, and this time, my dad had left in a rush without a real goodbye. It was hard for us to go alone, and my brothers and I never understood why he had left. We stayed two weeks in a cramped room with little food and only two suitcases of personal items. The only food we had was water, vegetables, fruits, and rice. The room was dark, damp, and small. We would play outside close to the house during the day but remained indoors after six. I remember feeling scared and a lot of the time, sick. In the evening, the other family and my family, though of different religions, sang hymns.

Finally, my mom decided to try to get us out of Zaire to America, to where my dad was. She walked to the American Embassy with the father of the family sharing our abandoned building. After showing her American Embassy ID, she was let into the compound. Inside, she begged for help out of the country. People there would not listen. Frantically, she was trying to insist that her children were American. Out of the blue, a family friend, who knew my mom through my dad, called her into her office. It was a miracle that she recognized my mom, but she felt eager to get us out of the country safely. She explained that our departure would be possible because my brothers and I had diplomatic passports. There was a flight the next morning.

The night before leaving, we said goodbye to the home, country, family, friends, life, and culture we knew and loved. It was hard for my mom to leave her mother and sisters because she knew it would probably be a long time before she saw them again. She worried for their safety, but there was no way they could get out. Even so, she was more afraid to put my brothers and me in any more danger.

The next morning we were on our way to a place unknown to us. We couldn't know how my father would react when he found out we were in the United States without his help. My mom cried most of the flight, so full of pain, regret, and loss. We landed at Reagan International Airport late the following day. My mom used a pay phone to inform my father and my Uncle Charlie about our arrival. I sat with my brothers and watched as my mom argued with my dad over picking us up. He was distressed to know that we had made it to America, and he was not willing to meet us. He didn't care. My uncle insisted on getting us.

The next year would turn out to be one of the roughest years my family had seen. We moved into a house that my uncle owned. My mom struggled to get a job, a car, enough money, and was having trouble from my father. My new American school was also a challenge. I had little English, and I had trouble communicating with my peers and teachers. But soon, I began picking up English and losing the language I was raised on, one of my biggest regrets.

After a year and a half of putting up with a new culture, language, way of life—and also the constant fighting between my parents—the biggest thing happened that would change our lives forever. My parents divorced, and my mom, my brothers, and I moved to St. Louis for a new start. The next few years were peaceful and easier.

Now, we live in Florida, and I am a boarding student at a private high school in St. Louis. I look back at my early years, and I appreciate the troubles we went through. Those years taught my family good lessons. We learned to appreciate what we have and never take for granted what home means. My mom's family keeps in touch through letters and phone calls, but I always sense a void in my mother's heart and a yearning to go home. One day we will all go back to visit our homeland.

Nicole "Nicky" Miezi Deprez, Zaire
St. Louis County Private High School

Ekapong Tangsaksathid

My hometown, Bangkok, is the capital of Thailand. It is a busy city much like New York City, with its massive population, skyscrapers, and crowded streets. It is this "big city" atmosphere and the fact that my entire family lives there which cause me to love Bangkok.

I was born in 1983 to my parents, Vitoon and Viyade Tangsaksathid. Together we lived in a six-story house with my two older brothers and older sister, as well as my grandmother and uncle. We have a family packaging business that was established by my grandfather.

As an adolescent, I thought only about playing and having fun, and I neglected my studies. I went to school in the early morning, not to study, but to play soccer! In the class, while completing assignments and taking tests, it was so hard for me to concentrate. I grew restless in my chair, wanting to go outside and play. Needless to say, I had poor study habits.

As I grew older and moved on to study chemical engineering at Burapha University, my attitude toward studying changed, and I began to take my studies more seriously. Moreover, my parents put their hope in me and my major to propel the family business to become bigger and stronger. After I earned my bachelor's degree, I made a big decision to go to America to pursue a master's degree. I arrived in New York City in 2006 and studied at LaGuardia Community College. It was a completely new experience for me, living alone, without my parents. Being by myself forced me to learn how to survive. Fortunately I was not entirely alone. In New York I met lots of fellow Thai people who offered me advice. However, there were so many things I needed to find out for myself about life and my new home, especially the American culture and behavior.

After studying English at LaGuardia for almost a year, I transferred to Fontbonne University in St. Louis, Missouri, to study in the master of business program. I got an opportunity to live in a dormitory on campus with American students, so not only was I learning business, but I was also learning closely about American life. Recently, I got an American girlfriend. She is nice, smart, and wonderful.

᠉ ᠉ ᠉

An Important Lesson

I am twenty-four years old now, and I have had many experiences. I am the youngest child in my family, and I have two older brothers and one older sister. Not only did we live together in a big house in the city, but we also had activities such as camping, hiking, and swimming, which took us out into the countryside. We were so happy, although sometimes we had small fights.

I have numerous happy memories of my childhood, but I have one significant memory which impressed me deeply. When I was in elementary school, I got very low grades. My GPA was less than 1.5, and I got Fs in many subjects. My father and my mother were so angry, and my father became very annoyed. He decided to hit me fifteen times.

After I was hit one time, I started crying because it hurt. When my father hit me the fifth time, my older brother came over and stopped my father. He offered to take the punishment instead of me. My brother said it was his fault because he did not teach me well.

At that time, I felt sorry for my brother, but my father still hit him. My father's reason for continuing to hit my brother was to make our sibling relationship stronger so that we would care for and help each other more and more.

After that incident, I studied hard. I did not want my brother to get hit again. Even though my father punished and blamed me, I still love and respect him, and I think it was a good lesson for me and my brother. Whatever I can do for my family, I will do it.

Ekapong Tangsaksathid, Thailand
MBA Graduate Program, Fontbonne University

Petr Kholodner

Iwas born in 1922 in a small town in Belarus, a part of the former Soviet Union. My father passed away when I was seven, so our mother brought up my younger brother and me.

In 1939, after leaving high school, I entered the Moscow Railway Institution. However, on September 1, 1939, there was a new law according to which every eighteen-year-old boy who finished high school had to go into the army. I was drafted and sent to military school. When I finished the military school in 1941, the invasion of the German army began. During World War II, I served as a combat officer until 1944, when I was wounded and lost an arm. After the war, I finished law school and worked as a lawyer.

Since January 1993, I have lived in St. Louis with my daughter and her family.

Tales from the Cemetery

The city where I was born and grew up had a large Jewish community because in the old times it was a part of the Jewish Pale. It meant that only Jewish people could live in this area. The community had a special funeral team that helped families to bury the body if someone passed away. All members of the team were volunteers. There was no payment. To be a member of the team was a great honor. However, everyone who wanted to join the team had to pass a test.

My grandfather, a tall, thin, strong man with a black beard and mustache, was a member of the funeral team, and he often told me of curious events. I remember two of them.

A young man who wanted to join the team received his task. At midnight he should go to the cemetery and hammer in a stake in a grave. The young man took a stake and a hammer and went to the cemetery. It was cold, dark, and windy. He imagined he heard voices and saw ghosts behind the tombstones. Dripping with sweat, he reached the selected grave and quickly hammered in the stake. But when he tried to leave the place, he could not move. He was sure that the deceased in the grave was holding the hem of his overcoat. In great fear he called for help. When the members of the team came running, they found out that the young man had fastened the hem of his overcoat to the grave with the stake!

The second story was about another man who wanted to join the same team. He got a different task for his test. He had to go to the cemetery and make soup! So he did. That day he prepared all the things he would need, and at midnight he went to the cemetery, set on the fire, and began to cook. When the soup started boiling, he noticed a strange creature coming from the darkness. It looked like a ghost wearing a white shroud. Instead of a head there was a skull. The ghost approached slowly and noiselessly. The man began shivering. The ghost came closer, then stopped and stretched out his arm in the man's direction. The man spooned up a full scoop of soup and poured it over the stretched-out hand. The ghost uttered a yell and disappeared into the darkness. The next day there was a meeting of the team. The man was accepted as a new member. Everybody shook hands with him. But the chairman shook with his left hand. His right hand was bandaged.

I was a seven-year-old when I heard these stories. I was very proud of my grandfather and his friends, and I wished I were a member of the team. In my imagination I became a hero too. But at night in the darkness, when I went to bed, I lost all my bravery and hoped I would never have to go to the cemetery.

Petr Kholodner, Belarus
Parkway AEL Program

Esteban Xifré Villar

The day of my birth, there was great agitation in my family. My parents, Eugenio and Rocio, had been married for seven years, and my grandparents were getting a little anxious as to when their desired grandchild was going to come. Actually, I should say *granddaughter* because both of my grandmas longed, more than anything, for a little girl that they could take care of. That might have been the reason why, when I was first presented to the whole family, my grandma started screaming with great excitement, "Es una nena! Es una nena!" (which means, "It is a girl! It is a girl!"), only to be slightly disappointed to know that the pink sheet in which I was wrapped had been used because there were no blue ones left in the hospital.

I was received into a caring and loving family in which my parents did all they could to provide all the best for their children. Even though we were not rich, I never had a single moment in which I lacked something I needed. My dad and mum worked really hard all day long so that nothing necessary would be missing. I remember when I was little staying every day after school with my grandparents until mum and dad would get back from work. Each day that I stayed at my Grandma Merita's, I played with my friends down the street—soccer and action figures were favorites—and that's where I met another boy with my same name. It was shocking to me since I didn't know two people could have the same name! This was inconceivable to my young, immature way of looking at the world. I was soon to learn that there were a lot of things I didn't know yet. I look back at experiences like this and wish I had always kept that childlike, innocent, free-of-responsibility way of living, oblivious to the demands that grown-ups have.

I was enrolled in one of the best schools in Montevideo during kindergarten and the first years of elementary school. It was always made clear to me, however, that I should value all that I had and never take anything for granted. Values and moral standards are very important in our family, and I remember growing up looking up to my parents and longing to one day be as fair, intelligent, and hardworking as they were.

My sister, Ifigenia ("Ifi"), is two years younger than me, and I remember growing up with her, playing in my backyard with our dog and chasing her around. Even from her very early years, she was always the quiet, proper, and almost lady-like girl, and I was the unbearable kid that ran around the house. (Things have changed a little bit since then. . . .)

When I was in third grade, my sister and I changed schools to another one closer to home. Around this time my little brother was born. He was named Emanuel, which means "God with us," and he became the center of attention for the whole family. It was a difficult time for our family, since my parents were abandoning the little kiosk in which they worked to focus on their particular professions. In addition to this, Ifi and I were both terrified about going to a different school. Also, the economic situation of Uruguay was shaky, and that was altering our daily lives. My brother seemed to my parents as an angel sent from God in such changing and uncertain times—repose and joy in the midst of many difficult situations.

As I went through school and high school, I made a lot of friends, matured a little, and learned to be more modest and humble in my speech and actions. I was a pretty good student, but I had a hard time disciplining myself and organizing my time. I never stopped singing and playing a lot of sports—these being the things that I am really passionate about.

It wasn't until winter of 2004 that I first heard about a private boarding high school in St. Louis through a friend who had lived in the United States and sent her daughter to this school. It was at first a wild idea to think that one day I could go to school in a different country, but my sister never stopped hoping that it might be possible for us both to go. This high school experience has been one of the biggest blessings in my life.

I am currently enrolled at Principia College, after graduating from high school. I am a freshman, and college life is just starting to make sense to me. I have tons of expectations for what's to come. I don't really have a plan as to how the next few years are going to be like. I'm not like that. I just let it develop.

It is amazing what can happen when we let life surprise us.

A Tent Tale

We always knew what we were doing during the summer. As soon as Christmas and New Year's were done with, and the heat of the summer* started to increase, our family would get a few things together and go camping. The particular camp we went to was owned by the government, and it was specifically meant for public school teachers and their families. Since my mum was a teacher, we took advantage of this opportunity.

The camp had several positive things. First, it was relatively affordable since salaries for teachers were not very high, and that was taken into consideration. Also, it was not too far from home, so sharing the ride with my two siblings in the back seat of the car wasn't unbearable. In addition to this, the most important thing of all was that a lot of teachers were young, and they had kids. Most of the time, the kids were either my age or my sister's or my brother's, so we would always find friends to hang out with.

Life was simple. It consisted of going to the beach, playing soccer and volleyball in the sand, helping my parents prepare meals, and staying up really late at night playing cards and chatting with friends about everything that came to mind. No pressure, no time. Relaxing and having fun were the only rules.

*Note: Summertime is flipped from what it is in the northern hemisphere. At home in Uruguay, the summer months are from mid-December until halfway through March. January is, however, the hottest month of them all, and it was then that we would always go camping.

The first year we went to this camp, we didn't have much experience on what it was like, so we decided to stay in the cabins that were available. We learned pretty soon, however, that space was really restricted inside, with only one room to sleep and cook. Taking our own tent was the way to go. We could set it wherever we wanted and take as much space as we desired, so long as we didn't disturb the other campers.

Considering ourselves capable enough to handle it, our second year we borrowed a tent from a family friend. He told us it was big and had a stable structure—just a little difficult to put together, but comfortable and water-resistant. Being the dexterous campers that we were, we chose a perfect, shady location that everyone else seemed to have missed. The terrain was slanted, but we decided (upon our extensive knowledge of the subject) that it did not matter where we put up the tent, and the rest of the people had just skipped this outstanding site.

We worked hard all day to put the tent together. Its structure proved to be very intricate to assemble, and finally we got to the point where we just wanted to get done with it. It might be important to remark that our tent did not look anything like what other people had. It was not aerodynamic whatsoever; it was more like a huge house where walls and roof had been replaced by water-resistant fabric. It had two separate rooms, and a person could stand inside it (and even stretch his hands a little) with no problem. By the end of the day, we were pretty proud of our work, even though the tent looked a little bent to one side and kind of old compared to the brand new ones that were all around us. We were content with the fact that that night, we would sleep safely, enjoying the fruits of our labor.

Our happiness, though, was going to be shaken—in a big way—pretty soon. The second or third day we were there, it began to rain softly as nighttime approached. We were tired from the day, so we went to bed reasonably early. Little did we know that that was just the beginning of a very long night.

As the night progressed, the wind picked up, and the tent began to make strange noises and to move in a way that even we could tell was not normal. Water (coming down the slope) started to enter through the space that was left between the ground and the bottom of the tent. At this point, we all woke up. We were terrorized since, by now, the wind was unbearable. Light posts outside kept turning off and on due to the force with which the wind was shaking the wires connected to them. The sharp sound of the wind passing through the trees and leaves kept making me doubt the strength of the pines that surrounded us.

Suddenly, our gigantic tent could not take the strength of the wind anymore. A whole lateral part came off the ground. Immediately everyone got up and grabbed one of the sticks that were dug into the soft ground. It was clear that our tent would not resist for very long without our support. Even then, the wind proved to be too much for us to put up with. Another section came off the floor, and by now the fabric was dancing around, inviting the wind to come inside, where it had more surface to push our tent up and away. Unfortunately, there was not much we could do about it. Despite our efforts, the cover came off, and we stayed there holding the iron sticks while all our stuff was getting wet.

What I remember most about this experience was my father. He stood there in the middle of the tent grabbing onto whatever he could as he told the rest of us what to do. Until the very end, he did not let go, and at the very pinnacle of the experience, when the tent was about to fly off, he yelled, "Dios esta con nosotros!!!" (God is with us), which made me hold on even tighter to the stick I was responsible for. That night, he appeared as a hero. Much bigger than any movie superhero, he was a real one, and he was my dad.

We spent that night in the "communal center" with some other families that had suffered similar fates to ours. Sleeping by the fireplace, after having moved all our stuff indoors, was the biggest pleasure that I remember at that time.

We learned to laugh about this experience once it was over. Mum found it particularly funny that my dad was yelling like a madman in the middle of the night about God protecting us. To me, however, it was a heads up to recognize the kind of family I had and to become convinced that I had the best dad in the world.

That night will always stay with me, for it taught me a lot about courage, devotion, and poise during difficult situations. Without a doubt, my dad is the living example of these qualities that I hope to see reflected in my experience.

Esteban Xifré Villar, Uruguay
Principia College

Huilan Wang

My name is Huilan. I was born at midnight in the late autumn, 1965, in the city of Zigong, China. I had a big family, and I was the youngest among my parents' six children. My schooling was typical, elementary school through college. After that, I worked for fifteen years. My first job was a manager in a company in Zigong, and then I worked for the media in Chengdu and Beijing.

I have been writing since I was twenty. My first work was published in 1986, and my first poetry collection, *The Red Candle*, was published in 1994. During the intervening turbulent years, I wrote a number of articles and reports.

I have received many awards for my poems. I was one of the winners in the National Poetry competitions in 1990, 1993, and 1994 in China. During my fifteen working years, my poems, prose, stories, plays, and reports have appeared in many Chinese magazines and newspapers. I am also a regular contributor to *China News Digest* in the United States. I have four published collections of poems, prose, and reports in Chinese. Among them, *The Career of Youth* and *The Report on China's Education* were on the best-seller lists in 1997 and 1998.

I came to the United States in 2001, and I currently live in St. Louis with my immediate family. I am honing my English skills while continuing my studies in college. I plan to write in both Chinese and English in the future.

The Red Bean

The Red Bean

The red bean grows in the South
Its sparse sprouts weave
    with spring
Glean some more for me, I pray
So that you'll see
It's the sign
    of remembrance.

This is an ancient Chinese poem. It is very famous in China. I read this poem for the first time when I was nine. From that time, I wanted to become a poet. And how I longed to have a red bean, a real poet's red bean! After all, what was a poet without a real red bean?

I kept asking my classmate Xiaoyan for one. However, she had only one herself, and she would only smile and say "Sorry" to me each time I asked. We were in elementary school. Xiaoyan was a farmer's daughter, but all the rest of the children lived in the city. The teacher told us Xiaoyan was living with her aunt because her parents had died. The first time she came to our classroom, she wore a very dirty and shabby skirt. She wanted to take a seat, but everyone told her that the seat had been taken. Then Xiaoyan tried to change to another row and another seat. While she was walking near me, I just said, "You can sit near me if you want." She sat near me without saying a word.

Xiaoyan was good at all her subjects. Soon we became friends. Every day we walked to class and back home together. We were happy. Time passed. A new term was beginning. One day when we were climbing a mountain, Xiaoyan got so tired that she could not move a step further.

She dropped to the ground, and tears rolled down her cheeks. Just then I caught up to her. I sat down by her side, took out an apple, and offered it to her as I usually did. However, she refused it.

"What's happening to you?" I asked.

"I am thinking this is the end," she answered in a soft, small voice.

"I won't ask you for the red bean anymore, I promise you, but don't cry," I continued to say to her. After a while, she told me she wanted to go home, and she would like to see her parents very much. The next day, things were even worse. Xiaoyan did not come to class. It had never happened before, so I worried and ran to her aunt's house at break time. In a small and dark room, Xiaoyan was lying on her bed. Her face was pale, and her lips were white. Clearly she was very sick, and she was dying. Her eyes fell on me, and she motioned me to come nearer. With an effort, she stopped her tears and smiled at me. She took out the red bean from her lovely box and passed it to me.

"This red bean was my mother's. She left it to me before she was gone. She wanted me to become a poet. Now, I want you to keep it." She took a very long time to say these words. These were her last words. I cried as if my heart would break. I lost my best friend at that moment.

Three days later, I took my first poem to Xiaoyan's little mound. I did not cry. I just read my poem to her quietly:

I'm coming, little maid
With a warm flame laden
With the fruit from the trees
With the grain from the fields

Every little stream is lively
All the orchard trees are golden
And on each small and waving shoot
Hangs your dream.

Huilan Wang, China
Parkway AEL Program
St. Louis Community College
Webster University

Paula Jones

I was born May 1, 1977, in Mexico City, where traditions mix with daily life. I grew up in Oaxaca, in a family dedicated to work and study. My father was an economist dedicated to his job and personal life. My mother, a strong woman, has been the support for my sister, my brother, and me.

Interested in the study of law, I enrolled in the Universidad Autonoma de Mexico, where I attended law school through the seventh semester. I developed an interest in becoming an international lawyer, which required that I speak two languages. Therefore, I decided to move to the United States for six months.

I moved to a wonderful little town named Silverthorne, Colorado, where I met my husband, Joshua Jones. After a year of being together, our lives changed when we discovered that we were going to have a baby. Her name is Sofia.

My parents-in-law offered to help us pay for our school, so we moved to St. Louis, Missouri, where we are attending St. Louis Community College.

Journey through My Childhood
My Poor Little Town

We lived in Oaxaca, a poor little town close to the ocean. Every morning when I woke up, I saw out of my window the immense blue ocean.

I would get dressed and run toward the water. I loved when the fresh wind touched my face and brought little breezes to me. Each grain of sand looked like a brilliant diamond. The waves were slender and light and somewhat impassive. During the night they dressed up with glamour and elegance. Our community worked the land. Every morning the man of the family dug the land and tried to persuade her to make her best job. I remember we shared the vegetables we grew. Each day, my mother and I visited some of our neighbors.

Lola was my favorite neighbor. She looked like her hens, brimming and coquettish with joy. However, sadness lived in her eyes. She had no family. I don't know all her story, but one son drowned as he was crossing the river into the United States. Singing and dancing were how Lola forgot the bitter flavor of her loneliness. Her day started with the sound of music. To the sound of her music she was feeding her fat hens and ugly pigs. When the light fog of the morning touched our bodies, my mother and Lola exchanged greetings—and vegetables.

Coquita was a quiet woman. Her silence was as tranquil as her own moves. She looked like a refined turkey. She was the best cook in my little town. I loved to spend the afternoons in her aromatic kitchen. Vegetables and meats covered her pots and frying pans. The smells of her food jumped and played through the entire village.

Panchito and Cleo were a sweet couple. They had a little store, named Patio of My House. Their store was like a warm sweet potato. Patio of My House had a little of everything, from candy and chocolates to a diversity of refreshments. Their bread was their masterpiece. That was what I loved the most. Flour covered Panchito from head to foot. Every afternoon his bread was ready for people to take home.

In the afternoons, when the whole village breathed the air of tranquility, the houses opened their doors. The people scattered colored chairs everywhere and spent their time between laughter and gossip. Meanwhile, pots of coffee boiled and jumped and waited for those lovers of good grain. The smell of those hours in my town was of an ocean tired of waiting for the moon. The night sprinkled the sky with little grains of sand. Everybody there was like a big family.

My House, My Garden, My Tree

My house was as simple as bread and butter. Two rooms, the kitchen, and a little living room were the whole of my house. But the garden was my favorite part of my house. Flowers, small strawberry patches, hens, chicks, roosters, and Guicho, my dog, were the residents of my garden. With its different kinds of trees my garden was the best in town. A few of the trees were too tall for me, and it was impossible to get their fruit. The smallest trees were robust and tipsy like my grandmother. They didn't have fruit, but they looked nice in my garden.

But one of the trees was my favorite. It was in back of my house. Huge and imposing—the biggest tree in town—it was still a humble tree, and for all its humility, it was a little shy. Its branches were long and strong. Together we spent the afternoons. It was part of my privacy. Given that I had to share my room with my sister, it was like my second room. It was my best friend. It waited for my arrival home from school, and it listened to me. The afternoons did not have an end. Together we contemplated the sunset, which brought with it a heap of furious red ants. The red ants took possession of my tree. More than one climbed up my pants, ready to attack. When they arrived, I prepared my departure to my room.

The First and Only Telephone in My Town

One morning, when I was seven years old, doubt patrolled my town. Something strange and different had come. I remember the people were meeting in the plaza of town. The old people were dismayed. The religious women walked in groups like gossiping hens. The surprised priest accompanied the religious to see the new artifact. Among little bashful laughter, everyone went toward the place where the devil of technology had taken root.

Tomas Perez was the fortunate (or disgraceful!) one who had for the first time accepted this technology into his funny red house. The telephone sat on a pretty little table in the living room, surrounded by branches of fresh roses and little pieces of porcelain china. It seemed to have more importance than anything there.

Days passed, and the people started to know the mystery of the telephone. They learned to make use of it faster than anybody imagined. To receive and make calls was the telephone's service. Proud of its duty, it rang day and night. Its sound was better than the singing of a sparrow.

The whole town was happy. Tomas and his telephone were good business. Lucas was Tomas's younger son. Lucas painted each day with a different color. But one day his father decided on a new color for Lucas. He would become Tomas's assistant. Faster than a lightning bolt, Lucas and his fast bicycle went from house to house announcing new calls. People entered and exited the funny little house all day and some nights. The telephone put an end to the privacy of the Perez family.

My Wonderful Parents

My mother was a small woman full of legends: legends that spilled a little of themselves to each generation, legends that pierced time. Sundays in the mornings, with a little delicate puff in my ear, my mother woke me up with a legend. As we lay together in bed, the words went whispering little by little until the legend finished. Afterwards, small and light like an ant, my mother with nimble moves prepared the best breakfast for her family.

My father was a good man. Short and a little fat but very strong, he looked like a brown little bean. His face was like a full moon and his eyes small, like buttonholes. The soles of his feet were more dry than the desert. He wore an ugly brown hat all the time, but it didn't look bad on him. He was the best peasant I have ever seen in my life. He loved to work our land. When he came back from work, he told us how life was beautiful. He said he didn't have any reason to feel bad because God gave to him everything he needed: a wonderful family and our land. That place signified for my father a gift from God.

My Dog Guicho

My dog, Guicho, was very ugly, but very good. He belonged. My father confided in Guicho more than anyone else. They were more than friends.

When dinner was ready, the first ones in the kitchen were my father and his dog. From time to time my father shared his food with his friend. Sometimes my father gave him a piece of meat with his mouth. My mother told my father again and again that wasn't good, but my father didn't care. One day Guicho bit more than the piece of meat from my father's mouth. My father's lip was bleeding, and my mother laughed while she cleaned my father's lip.

When the sun touched the moon, Guicho ran toward the hill, waiting for my father to return from work. Every day at the same time Guicho followed the same routine, until one day, he waited, but my father did not come back from work. Guicho waited on the hill until the next morning, but his wait was in vain. The next morning the whole town was in mourning. Guicho did not stop his routine for more than six months. But he was tired, and the sadness weakened him.

My poor little town and everybody in it have been little lights in my life. My memories are the inspiration of my life.

Paula Jones, Mexico
St. Louis Community College

Sonia Shazadi

Sonia's Memory of Home
(as dictated to her ESL teacher)

Hi, my name is Sonia Shazadi, and I am from a village outside Lahore, Pakistan. I moved here in November 2001. I have two sisters and one brother, a mother, father, and nine cousins living with us in St. Louis. I want to tell you about my memory of Pakistan.

Our house was made of bricks and clay. We had tall walls around the house and one gate with two doors. We lived close to a farm. My family and many relatives worked on this farm. My mom and I took food and water to the workers. Sometimes we carried the food on our heads. I would kneel down and she would put the food on my head. We would wrap a scarf around our heads to help carry a clay pot of hot rice. My mom carried a silver pot of water on her head. People sat in the shade of a tree to eat. We had cows and sheep in a field, chickens around the house, and goats outside, tied to an apple tree. In a field we grew carrots, gheia tori, onions, tomatoes, turnips, cauliflower, peppers, bitter gourd, corn, ginger, and wheat. Some of the fruits we grew were peaches, watermelon, apples, and coconut. I wish we still lived close to a farm.

Sometimes I helped my family cut the corn or pick the fruits and vegetables. Then we washed them with well water. The well was down in the ground. We had to pump the water out. My mom had a clay oven to cook the food. We put sticks in there to build a fire. We put our food on plates that our mom wove from corn leaves. If it was raining, we ate

inside. When it was nice weather, we ate outside on the ground, or on our beds, which were woven cots.

I remember the smell of my mom's chicken cooking in the clay oven outside. My favorite dish was one my mom cooked with carrots, peas, and potatoes together with many spices. It smelled so good! We drank milk from the cows. My mom put the milk in a special jar with salt and put it outside overnight. The next day we had to shake it up. Then we could drink it.

There was a special room in our house. Many families had this. In there was an American bed, some chairs, pretty pictures, and other nice things. This room was usually locked. Only my mom could open it. We used it when guests, like religious people, came to visit. There was a window between this room and the window in another bedroom. My sisters and I tried to open both windows so we could see all the pretty things in this room.

Sonia Shazadi, Pakistan
Fifth Grade, Parkway Elementary School

Soo-Gil Yang

I was born in Seoul, South Korea. I passed my childhood ordinarily. My parents were faithful Christians, so I went to church, naturally. Up until now I believe in God and Jesus Christ.

I graduated as an industrial engineer from my university. After finishing college, I joined the army as an armored forces officer. At that time I married my wife, an army nurse. (This year in June will mark our eighteenth wedding anniversary.) I worked for a motor company in the production control department. After that, for some time I owned my own business selling tools and repairing spray-paint booth equipment.

My wife wanted to study more about her field, and we decided to come to the United States. Today, my older son is in ninth grade, and my younger son is in seventh grade. My wife is also a student. She is studying for a Ph.D. in nursing at Saint Louis University.

I love music and sports, especially tennis and golf. I like to study English, too.

Moving Day

I remember a day when I was a young boy, maybe six years old. I was a first-grade elementary school student. My family lived in a riverside house. Of course, we rented it. At that time, most people did not have their own house. My father had just bought a new apartment for the first time in his life.

When the morning came to move, my father asked me, "Can you find our new home? Here, this coin is for you. After school you should ride the bus and come to our apartment." He gave me careful directions.

However, I did not pay attention to his words. I went to school, took my classes, and got engaged in conversation with my friends about my family's moving. When the school day finished, I rode the bus and got off at the stop I thought was right. But something was wrong. It wasn't the correct street. There were many buildings, cars, and people. I just wandered here and there. After about two hours' wandering, I realized I was lost. I cried and cried. The sun went down, and darkness was all around. It began to frighten me that now I would be an orphan with no home. I was hungry and exhausted.

Suddenly, a gentleman came to me and asked me, "Why are you crying? Where is your house? Do you know your telephone number?" Still crying, I told him everything I knew. The gentleman took me to a small restaurant and gave me some bread and a cup of milk. I ate it all, and I felt a little bit more comfortable than before. He listened carefully about my actions. Then, he took me to my old house. When we arrived there, my uncle had been waiting there all afternoon. He had been very worried. Thank God! I couldn't help crying again as I rushed to him.

Now I remember how kind the gentleman was. However, I don't remember his face. I want to know about him, but I can't. I hope that he is healthy and happy somewhere, now and forevermore. God bless him! I learned that to pay attention is very important when someone talks to me!

Soo-Gil Yang, Korea
International Institute

Fehima Kurtic

My name is Fehima Kurtic. I was born in Bosnia on April 24, 1960, along with my twin brother. Unfortunately he died when he was six months old. I was raised with two older sisters and one younger brother. Also, in Bosnia I finished high school. After high school I worked as a dressmaker for a company.

My husband, two children and I came to the United States late in December 1998, because of the horrible war in my country. Here in St. Louis, I was employed by Alco for five years and worked as an assembler.

Now I am studying English at the International Institute in St. Louis. I am satisfied. I have a good life with my husband and two children.

Red Dog

Although there were many interesting things that happened in my childhood, one which I will always remember is the story about my red dog.

I had many good friends in my neighborhood. I also had a white puppy. My puppy was very cute and very interesting. My friends and I loved to play with him. One day my friends and I got into a fight. They said a lot of bad things about me and about my puppy. They said that my dog looked ugly because white is not pretty for a dog.

When my parents went to work that day, I found red paint in my basement, and I poured it all over my dog! When my parents came

home, they started laughing. They told all my family about my crazy idea. Even today, thirty-five years later, when we remember what I did, we all laugh as if it just happened.

Fehima Kurtic, Bosnia
International Institute

Congxin "Nicky" Liu

I was born in 1979 in Guizhou, a southwestern province of China, and I am the only child in my family. In my generation, each couple could have only one child because the Chinese people were required to reduce the birthrate due to the large population.

When I was eleven years old, my family moved to a beautiful garden city in eastern China. I finished my elementary, middle, and high schools there. After I graduated from high school, I went to a university and majored in broadcast art. Later, I became a news anchor at the television station. I was an entertainment news anchor for about three years.

I have been in the United States for two years. I lived in Boston when I first came to this country because my husband was studying at Boston University at that time. After my husband graduated, we moved to Raleigh, North Carolina, in January 2004. Then, in November 2004, we came to St. Louis because my husband got a job here.

I am going to Webster University this summer, and my major will be media communications. I have met a lot of friends from different countries in St. Louis, and I hang out with them sometimes. I enjoy my life in St. Louis!

My Mountains

I was born in a small village surrounded by big mountains. In my memory, it was the most beautiful place I've ever seen. The mountains

were green all the time. There were colorful flowers all over the mountains every spring.

I liked to climb the mountains with other kids when I was a little girl. We spent all of our afternoons after school in the mountains. The lovely mountains were our close friends. They gave us beautiful flowers, delicious wild fruits, and a childhood of happiness.

I remember at that time we took a field trip every spring. We spent the whole day in the mountains. We kept climbing and climbing until we reached the summit. From the summit, we saw yellow broccoli flowers all over the ground; they looked like a yellow carpet. We felt and smelled fragrant blasts of wind. What a nice day! We played games, sang, and ate snacks. Before sunset we went back home. I knew dinner was waiting for me. After dinner I told my mother about our journey while I fell asleep.

I still miss my mountains. They are in my dreams wherever I go. They are always reminding me of my childhood.

Congxin "Nicky" Liu, China
Parkway AEL Program
Webster University Graduate Program

Cipriano Casado

I am from Argentina. I was born in Azul, a small town in the middle of the Pampas, in the province of Buenos Aires. There was not much to do there, but since my father was crazy about birds, we had all kinds of feathered animals in the backyard of our home. My job was to feed and clean them. I had three younger sisters, but of course they were exempt from the bird breeding chores. Years went by with the same routines.

Luckily, one day after a vacation, my parents decided to sell everything in Azul and move to a wonderful ski resort town in the south, in Patagonia: Bariloche. My father had leased a small, twenty-five-room bed and breakfast there. I was thirteen. By then, my toy of choice was a globe, and I would spin it, close my eyes, and put my index finger on it to see where I would travel, at least in my imagination. I loved maps, countries, history, and geography.

One day, as I was walking in the halls of my secondary school, I saw a pamphlet about a student exchange program sponsored by my school. I quickly signed up—without my parents' knowledge—and was selected to spend a year in Creve Coeur, Missouri, with an American family. I was barely sixteen. I couldn't believe it: one year in the United States, all expenses paid! I certainly did not know where Creve Coeur was, though I found out later it was a St. Louis suburb. My parents were not very happy about my idea, but with the help of some of their friends, they agreed to let me go. I became a senior at Parkway North High School, and the family I stayed with was fabulous. I had the best year of my life, no doubt! I learned English and lots about the culture.

A year, I felt, wasn't enough. As I was returning to Argentina, I told my American father that one day I would come back. The travel bug

and the passion for learning about other cultures and places were in me. I went to college in Argentina, graduated with a political science and international affairs degree, and ten years after that amazing experience in Creve Coeur, I came back in 1991 to pursue a master's degree at Washington University. I had the opportunity to work here, and one thing leading to another, I stayed in St. Louis, the city that so warmly embraced me in my adolescence. I worked in sales first and then decided I wanted to teach and spend time with kids. I have been a teacher since 1999.

I have traveled throughout the United States, including Alaska, by motorcycle, my other passion. In 1997, I even took the Pan Am Highway from St. Louis to Argentina (five months and 13,000 miles) on my motorbike! I am now a Spanish teacher at a private St. Louis high school and am married to Celina, a violin teacher and an amazing woman.

Buckets of Frogs

I grew up on a little farm outside of Azul, a small town in the Argentine Pampas. My Grandma Sara raised my sister Sabina and me because our parents both worked in town, sometimes until 7:00 p.m. There was no television in our house, and we did not have a telephone. Sabina and I spent most of our time outside on the farm, surrounded by a horse, two cows, two boxer dogs named Gundi and Estrella, chickens, pigeons, and rabbits. In the summertime, we picked peaches, figs, watermelon, grapes, and many kinds of plums. Here, on my childhood farm, is where my terror of frogs began . . . yes, frogs, and my little sister Sabina had a lot to do with that!

There was a big windmill near the house to pump our water, and next to it, my father had built an above-ground pool. There were a lot of gigantic frogs near there, and during the summer nights, they croaked continuously. Sabina loved these animals, and without my knowing, she would get a big bucket, go for a walk, collect frogs, and put them in the bucket. Later on, when I was distracted, she would come from behind me and literally dump over my head the bucket full of these horrendous, cold creatures. I panicked and screamed every time, while she laughed wholeheartedly.

I was maybe four or five years old. This happened all the time, and every time Sabina was "missing," I would hide because I knew what was coming. My parents and grandma repeatedly talked to her, trying to deter her from the "frog dumping," but to no avail. I was horrified by these creatures, and I still am.

A few years ago, while camping with friends near the Ozarks here in Missouri, I saw a big frog near me, and I instantly jumped up onto a camping table, without thinking. My friends were perplexed by my reaction. I had to explain my sister's adventures on our little Azul farm.

It is something I have a difficult time dealing with even today, and every time I see a frog, I think of Sabina and her bucket.

Cipriano Casado, Argentina
Parkway Public High School Graduate
Washington University MA, International Affairs

Pao-Chiang "Caesar" Huang

My name is Pao-Chiang Huang, but I am called Caesar. I was born in 1979 in Taipei, the capital city of Taiwan. There are four people in my family: my father, mother, younger sister, and I. When I was young (1979–1985), my parents were very busy in their work, so they put me in my grandparents' home. My grandparents lived in Gukeng Township, Yunlin County, a very small area in the countryside.

Later, when it was time to go to elementary school, I moved back to Taipei. I finished my education at Ming-Chuan University where I studied tourism. After that, I worked at the Formosa Hotel, and I also sold computers. As all young men in Taiwan, I did my military service.

I then decided to come to the United States to study English. I studied at George Mason University in Fairfax, Virginia. While I was studying there, I went with a church group to help clean up after Hurricane Katrina damaged New Orleans [in 2005].

I am now living in St. Louis and studying for my MBA at Fontbonne University. Living in St. Louis reminds me of the place where I spent my childhood because it is so green, and the people are friendly. For that reason, St. Louis is a great city for me.

Although my family is far away in Taiwan, I still can feel they accompany me all the time. I am thankful to my family members who taught me so many things. I will always keep them in my mind.

The Country Vs. the City

I was born in Taipei, Taiwan. When I was born, all my family members were very happy because I was a son. However, my parents were busy with their work, so they decided to put me in my grandparents' home. And for a while, that was my home, in the middle part of Taiwan.

My grandparents' home was located in a small country village where transportation was not very convenient. Therefore, every time we wanted to go to town, we had to wait about two hours for a bus. Although living there was not convenient, in my childhood I learned a lot of things. For example, I could distinguish what kinds of herbs could be eaten, how to catch birds without a net (and then, let them fly away), and how to make water guns from bamboo. My childhood there was vivid. Every day the only thing I had to do was play. However, when the time came for me to attend elementary school, my parents moved me back to Taipei, and I lived with them.

Living in Taipei was convenient, but the people there were not welcoming. Neighbors did not invite each other to their homes. People were always thinking about themselves. I disliked these kinds of attitudes. So my parents taught me how to hide my feelings, how to make friends with people I didn't like at first, and how to help people that needed my help. From my parents I learned valuable lessons, and I made a lot of friends from other places. Even now, I remember many of the things my parents taught me.

There is an old saying from John Milton that can explain my feelings: "The childhood shows the man, as morning shows the day."

Pao-Chiang "Caesar" Huang, Taiwan
MBA Graduate Program, Fontbonne University

Fartun Abdimalik

I was born on October 29, 1985, in a small city in Somalia called Brava. My grandmother took me with her when I was two years old. My grandma and I moved to another city in Somalia, Hamer, with my aunt and my cousins. At that time my mother was pregnant with my little brother. She was very sick, and I was giving her a hard time. My mother had three older children. Since I was the youngest one, I was the one who gave lots of trouble.

When my grandma and I moved to Hamer, my parents and siblings moved to Kenya because the war in Somalia was getting bad. I really didn't know my parents and siblings until I moved to Kenya when I was nine years old. After four years, we came to America. I started middle school in the sixth grade.

I got married when I was sixteen years old. I was in ninth grade. I had my first baby when I was in tenth grade and my second baby when I was in twelfth grade. I have been living in the United States for seven years and am now a college student. I love living in the United States.

Hijab

Hijab is the scarf that all Muslim women should wear. Hijab is very important for all women because it is in the Qur'an that Muslim girls and women have to wear the hijab.

Women wear hijab because Allah wants women to hide their beauty. When women wear hijab, it hides 70 percent of their beauty, so no men will bother them. It also means respect for their religion. All girls and women should wear it, no matter if they are married or not. I think it is very important that all women wear the hijab in the proper way. There are some women who wear the hijab half on their head. They don't cover all their hair. And that is not good. If the women are wearing hijab, they should cover their entire hair. This is my opinion, and it also says this in the Qur'an.

Girls should start wearing hijab when they are seven years old. The Muslim religion says that the seven-year-old will get used to it, if she starts wearing it at seven. I started wearing the hijab when I was six years old. I loved wearing it, even before I was six. In Somalia all women wear hijab, and I wanted to wear it too. At that time, I was living with my grandmother. She wouldn't let me wear it. She told me that I was too young. I cried when my grandmother took the hijab from me. She told me that I would make it dirty because I used to drag it on the floor. Sometimes I would go to her dresser and get hijab when my grandmother wasn't there. I put all the clothes on the floor, and I never put them back. My grandmother used to yell at me, and even sometimes she would whup me.

"The hijab is way too big for you. You are not old enough to wear the hijab. Just wait and your time will come," she explained to me. I cried all the time. I wanted to be like other girls, who were older than me. They had to wear it. Now talking about it, I think it is funny that I wanted to wear hijab that badly.

Now I have a daughter who is three years old. She loves to wear hijab. Every time when I wear it, she wants to wear it too. I bought her some hijab that is only for children. It's very different from the adult ones. It doesn't fall on the ground. It stays on her head until she takes it off. But she doesn't like it. She wants the ones I wear. If someone comes to my house, they laugh at her because she wears it all the time. Even when she goes to the bathroom, she wears it. People say to me, "Your girl will become a good Muslim."

My mother says that my daughter takes after me when I was young. This is the way I was when I was a child. This tells me that I loved wearing hijab.

Fartun Abdimalik, Somalia
St. Louis Community College

Wonye Chang

My name is Wonye Chang. I'm from South Korea. I spent most of my time in Seoul, the capital of South Korea and the biggest city in Korea. It is huge, so I grew up in high buildings with many people.

I graduated from a foreign language high school, where I learned French and English. But these languages didn't interest me much. I thought that history and social work were more attractive. I liked to think about the way that people lived before, and why they lived the way they did. When I had to choose my major for university, my father said history would be very important at the time that North and South Korea reunited. I agreed with my father.

I studied not only history but also the teaching of history. After four years in university, I prepared for an examination to become a teacher in middle and high school. I passed the test and became a middle-school teacher near where I lived. I taught Korean history for five years. I wanted to share the pleasure of knowledge about history with my students. I also recognized the beauty of the Korean arts.

I visited the United States because my boyfriend lived in St. Louis and ran a restaurant here. We were engaged in 2003 and married in 2004.

When we were engaged, I was still teaching in Korea, so I had to work in Korea and just visit him on vacations. In November 2004, I decided to retire from teaching and to live in St. Louis. Now I am studying at the International Institute and looking for a job. I heard that this country is the land of opportunities. I hope I will find them.

My Lost Recorder

I remember an incident when I was eleven years old. I had a very hard music teacher. Whenever students in his class misbehaved, he stopped class to stare at those students. His bald head and his face turned red as he became angry. With a long stick, he hit the hands of every student that didn't listen to him or didn't do what he said.

Every student in his class had to learn the recorder, a musical instrument. To learn how to play it, we all had to bring our instruments if we had music class that particular day. One day before his class, I found that I didn't have my recorder. I checked every bag, but I couldn't find it. Maybe I lost it, or maybe I didn't bring it to school. I told my best friend. We worried about it together. I didn't know what to do. When the bell rang, and then class started, my face felt hot, and I was so scared. My teacher said, "Everyone who doesn't have a recorder should come in front of me."

I was so afraid, but I tried to stand up. At that moment, my best friend passed me her recorder, and then she went in front of the teacher. It all happened in a few moments. I saw my friend's face when she stood in front of the teacher. She was scared also. I knew that I should not be in my seat and should have passed her recorder back to her. But I just couldn't do it.

After all this, my friend was beaten and had to stand in the back of the classroom. I felt so sorry. I couldn't concentrate in the music class.

As soon as the class was finished, I ran to my friend and asked her why she did that. She said she did it because she loved me and we were friends. I cried when she said that, and she cried. We became closer after that happened.

When the new year came, we were not in the same classes anymore. We had our new friends. Later we went to different high schools and colleges. Now I don't know where she is and what she is doing. I hope I can see her again some day and thank her for what she did for me.

Wonye Chang, Korea
International Institute

Lucija Ivicevic

My name is Lucija Ivicevic. I was born in Kresevo, a small city of Croatia (formerly Yugoslavia), on January 1, 1968. I grew up with two brothers and one sister.

Until I was eight, I lived with my mom and my grandparents. During this time, my father was in Germany. He worked there and saved money for our new house. After eight years, our house was finished. We moved in, and our father could stay with us. This was the happiest part of my childhood, when we again lived all together.

I finished my education in my city: elementary, middle, and high school. After high school I wanted to learn more, and I graduated from a school for drafters in a city which was far from my home. After finishing, I couldn't find a job. For two years I worked many different small jobs. Finally, I found work as a drafter in a company.

A big shock for me came in 1991 when my father died. That year, war began in my country, too, and everything changed. In 1993 I moved to Germany, where I lived for seven years. In 1995 I married my husband, Pero Ivicevic. We have a son, Luka, who is seven years old. These two are my best friends and the most important people in my life.

In 2000 we arrived in the United States and began a new life, and I am very glad to be here. In my free time I take English classes at a community college and read books. I also enjoy cooking.

My New Bike

I was nine years old. My biggest wish was to have a bicycle. I had an old one, but I wanted a new and cool one. My parents said to me that I needed to wait until my birthday. However, I told them that I had saved enough money for a bike, and that my mom needed just to take me with her when she went to town.

One day my mom said, "Come on, honey. We'll go in shopping." We went into a big supermarket where they sold dresses as well as bikes. While she was looking for some clothes, I looked in the corner of the store where they kept the bicycles. There were many different kinds. I tried to touch and to ride some of the bikes just to see which was good for me, but the salesman did not allow that. I knew that I had to choose the perfect one because I wouldn't have any money for another one later. I begged my mother to help me. She spoke with the salesman, and he gave me a few bikes to try. At last I chose one, which I considered to be the best. And really, it was a cool bike! It had three speeds. This bike looked very nice, with blue and yellow colors. The yellow could glitter in the dark.

However, there was a big problem. That bike was really expensive, and I did not have enough money. With tears in my eyes, I looked at my mother and gave the bike back to the salesman. I knew that my mother couldn't help me. She had just enough money for what she had planned to buy. I was sad.

A moment later, I saw how my mother was talking with the salesman. She said that she didn't like the dress that she had just bought, and that she wanted to have the money back. I knew my mother had been waiting for a new dress for the whole year and now, because of my bike, she didn't want to buy it. She said very cheerfully, "Here is the money for your bike!"

I was impatient on my way home. I went straightaway to my friends. I was the happiest child in the whole world. The following Sunday, I was with my mother in church. All the time I looked at my mom. She was beautiful in her old dress.

Lucija Ivicevic, Croatia
St. Louis Community College

Aurelio Toth

Itchy Horns

I remember living in Veracruz
Visiting my abuela
My mom wanted to live there
but we couldn't

There were bulls in the corral
They were nice
but if they saw a stranger
They would knock down the gate
and chase him . . .

I liked to ride the bulls better than the horses
They went fast, but they didn't try to get me off
If I fell off,
they stopped
I miss them . . .

Now I will tell you something funny
I liked to sharpen their horns!
I used a metal file
The bulls liked it when I did that
Maybe their horns were itchy.

Aurelio Toth, Mexico
Fifth Grade, Parkway Elementary School

Satomi Tanaka

I was born in Fujieda City, Shizuoka Prefecture, on September 20, 1979. My father is an electrician, and my mother is an office worker. I have an older sister and a younger brother. I love to go out with my sister because she is always kind and very nice to me. My brother is so funny. He always makes me laugh. We live with our grandparents. My grandpa and grandma are also very kind and smart. They teach me so many things. I'm really lucky because I have such a wonderful family.

I went to Aojima Elementary School for six years. From my home to school, it took about thirty minutes on foot. But I enjoyed walking in the middle of the rice field with my friends. I was a class representative, so sometimes I talked in front of all the people in my school. It was good experience for me. My essay is a memory when I was an elementary school student.

After that I went to Aojima Junior High School for three years. I was on the softball team. I was a pitcher and a captain of our team. After I graduated from junior high, I attended Shimada High School. I belonged to the drama club. I was interested in backstage operations, so I was mainly in charge of lighting, stage setting, clothes, and so on. I thought I would like to study more about backstage work, so I went to Tokyo, and at a technical college I studied editing, lighting, how to operate a TV camera, and how to mix sounds. After graduating from college, I thought I would look for work at a TV station in Japan.

However, I love American movies, and I was eager to know the real American culture, so I decided to come to the United States. I love children, so I came here as an au pair. My host family was awesome! I was

lucky to get to know them. I could participate in every celebration, like Halloween, Thanksgiving, and Christmas. I could also take classes in English and in art while I was here.

Today, I teach Japanese, mathematics, and English to children in Japan. When I am free, I paint in oils. I am interested in art now, so I would like to go to Italy and study fine arts there. That is what I want to do next.

My Tree

I remember a time when I was a fourth grader. It was a beautiful fall evening. I was climbing up a tree, a big tree. It was on the playground near my elementary school. I just loved to climb up that tree. I invited my friends to my tree, and we climbed together. We hung a tire from a branch, and we made a ladder from it of rope. When I swung, my feeling was so good. We didn't go home until the sun went down that evening.

Every day after school we ran to the tree and climbed up. We tried to make the tree more of a house. The view from the top of the tree was very beautiful, especially the moment when the sun went down because everything turned orange and red—even my friends' cheeks.

One day we were climbing up the tree as usual. I saw a teacher walking toward us. The teacher came under the tree, and he yelled at us, "Don't climb the tree! Come on down—now!" I wanted to ask him why, but I couldn't because his face looked really mad. I just felt so sad. He also said, "Take these ropes and tire. You're never allowed to climb up this tree again—ever!"

We were very disappointed. We took the ropes and tire away. On the way home, we couldn't talk. I felt sad more than angry. After that, we never climbed up the tree again. We just looked at it. The next day, we found another great secret place.

Satomi Tanaka, Japan
Parkway AEL Program

Tijana Avramovic

My name is Tijana Avramovic. I was born on the 2nd of July, 1982, in Belgrade, in Serbia and Montenegro. In Serbia, I lived with my mother, Jelena, who is a kindergarten teacher, my father, Dragutin, who is a geology technician, and my sister, Zorana, who is a student. Zorana studies the Serbian language and literature. These people are the best family in the whole world and the most important support in my life.

I was a member of the Serbian National Rhythmical Gymnastics Team and competed in several major competitions. After that, I started dancing (jazz, hip-hop, and ballet) and competed in the European Championships. In Vienna in 2004, I won second place. In addition, I competed in the World Championships in 2004 in Hungary, where I won third place in modern dance. I was also in acting school, and I studied under one of the most famous teachers in my country, Miroslav Mika Aleksic.

I was encouraged to come to America by my dance teacher, Snezana Sikimic. She is my best friend. I won my competitions with her help. I came to the United States to improve my English and to learn more about different cultures. I am here as an au pair. My American family is great. The children are smart and cute, and my host mother is a wonderful person. I like them all.

My goal is to go to a university in St. Louis, but I cannot do that without a scholarship, so I have to work hard. Learning a second language is a challenge, but I have spirit and heart. I have learned that everything is possible if I believe in myself and work hard. I am going to do that! I appreciate the help of my teachers in ESL school. They are very nice, good people, and great teachers. That is all. I think that is enough.

Bad Times in Wonderful Summers

When I was a little girl, I got to live every summer with my grandparents in the most wonderful village in the whole world. This special little town in northern Serbia is called Banatski Karlovac, and when I spent my summers there, it had one playground, a small cinema, and one park with a lot of trees. I loved the times I lived in Banatski Karlovac because I spent all day outside. This made me happy because I was an extremely active little girl who never liked to sit down. I had a fantastic sense of freedom when I spent the summers with my grandparents.

Their house was comfortable, with two bedrooms, a living room, a kitchen, and a bathroom. We always ate in the living room at a big table. The air inside was clean and fresh because my grandma kept the windows open all summer long. She grew a lot of pretty flowers right outside the windows, so every time I inhaled, I enjoyed their fragrance.

If I wasn't playing with my friends in the village, I was usually with my grandpa. He was a big man with big hands. He looked so strong that I called him "the man of steel." I was proud because he was so much taller than I was. My grandpa was amazing to me. All my friends were scared of him, including all the village boys, who never tried to bother me. Grandpa and I had a great time playing cards. I tried to calculate quickly during our games because he said fast thinking was an important skill to master.

Although I liked my grandpa very much, there was one thing I didn't like to do with him—eat meals. The problem was that I didn't like to eat. I was very thin, and eating was a tedious job to me. In fact, I remember each of the meals served in Banatski Karlovac. These meals were so boring that I felt like they were a big waste of time. The bad part was that Grandpa never let me leave the table until I had finished all of my meal, even if I didn't like the food. Sometimes I cried for one hour and begged him not to make me eat one more mouthful, but it never helped.

He didn't listen to me, and I felt angry and frustrated. In fact, I felt like I would sit on my chair for the rest of my life! Often, I tried to find a moment when Grandpa wasn't looking, so I could put my food under Grandma's plate. I also waited for the moment when he might leave the table, but it never came. When he finished his meal, he always crossed his arms and watched TV or read the newspaper. I cried, rolled my eyes, and thought, "What should I do?"

After a while, I reluctantly picked up my spoon and ate. When I finally finished, Grandpa didn't look at me. He simply said, "You are free now. Goodbye!" Even though my face was red and fat like a frog's from crying, I felt as free as a bird.

To this day, I don't like to eat meals with my grandpa because he still gets angry if my plate isn't completely empty. Even if one crumb of bread remains on my plate, he will say, "Please, Tijana, eat that." Then I hear the familiar words from my childhood and see the look of wisdom in his eyes. "You have to find time to eat because your power comes from what you put into your mouth," he always reminded me. Now that I have grown up into a strong woman, I finally understand what he meant.

Tijana Avramovic, Serbia and Montenegro
Parkway AEL Program

Lengbiye Barafundi

I was born November 29, 1962, in Mbandaka (Congo DR), the third in a family of twelve. My father, now deceased, was a professional soldier.

I took my elementary and high schools around Congo, in different places depending on my father's assignment. I completed my bachelor's degree in administrative and political sciences at the University of Lubumbashi in Katanga Province (Congo) in 1988. Then, I worked at the Embassy of Congo in Lusaka (Zambia) from 1990 to 1999.

As refugees, we knew we were coming to the United States, but we did not know our destination. I found myself and my family in St. Louis by chance. I had never known about St. Louis as a city in Missouri until eight hours before we landed on August 10, 2004—to live here and to love it.

Currently, I am an assembly worker at Glideaway, a bed frame manufacturing company. I enjoy keeping myself busy by doing everything pleasant to improve my mind, such as reading, writing, watching television, listening to radio, interacting with people, and chatting with my wife and my four children.

Shinkolobwe

The small mining town of Shinkolobwe, in the Democratic Republic of Congo, would have survived if the Second World War had not occurred. Unlike other towns destroyed because involved in that war, Shinkolobwe was not a battlefield and was not bombarded, but it had passively played a vicious role in being the source of the cynically precious uranium, used to make the famous atomic bombs that destroyed Hiroshima and Nagasaki in Japan. The mine of Shinkolobwe was closed to comply with the series of measures and decisions taken to end the war. The shutting of the mine meant the future death of Shinkolobwe as a town and its disappearance from the world map.

Some twenty-five years after the closure of the mine, during the slow dying of the town, my family was living in Shinkolobwe. It resembled a ghost town where almost three houses out of five were abandoned, and people were living together with nature and wild creatures. As children, we played in the abandoned houses transformed into habitations for small wild animals.

I was about seven years old, when one afternoon I was playing in one of the abandoned houses in our neighborhood. There was a wasps' nest in the house, and I wanted to destroy it. I started to stone the nest. I was excited to see the wasps scattering while I was escaping them. I got bolder, drawing closer to their nest. I decided to destroy it. I ignored the risks. Nothing would have stopped me from daring and threatening the dreadful wild and stinging insects.

The inevitable happened . . . I was stung! I found myself on the floor, as if I had been violently thrown. I will never know how many wasps stung me. I screamed for help and managed to get out of the house. Alarmed, my mother came to my rescue. She noticed I was disfigured with a swollen face and a head almost doubled in size. She would have punished me for the risky game if my condition had not been deteriorating fast. Besides my swollen face and head, I had spots all over my body, and I developed a fever. I was rushed to the hospital where I was given injections. Back home, I went to sleep until the next day.

I never returned to play in the house where I had learned one of the unforgettable lessons of my life. For sure, I will never again visit Shinkolobwe, my ghost town, since it exists no more.

Lengbiye Barafundi, Congo
International Institute
Webster University

Tania Taranda

Iwas born on January 16, 1972, in Belarus, a part of the former USSR. My parents worked as engineers. I have one brother who is four years older than me.

In 1993, I graduated from Radiotechnical University in Minsk, Belarus. After graduation, I worked as a computer programmer in a small medical firm. In January 1995, I married a man who had studied at the university together with me. Our first daughter, Varvara, was born in Minsk in November 1995.

My family and I arrived in the United States in 2002. My husband found work here, so it was the reason we changed our country. Our second child, Paulina, was born in April 2003, in Waterbury, Connecticut. We lived in several different states on the eastern coast of the United States. Now we live in St. Louis County, and I like this area so much. I do not work in the United States. I have been studying English.

When I Was Eight Years Old

When I was eight years old, I looked like an obedient little girl, but this was not true. I had long light blonde hair that my mother carefully styled into a neat braid every morning—but by evening, I always had a crow's nest on my head! Too, I had a bad temperament; I was extremely obstinate, and I had an opinion for every question. I always thought

myself to be right, and I also considered myself quite pleasant. I now realize that I was a very difficult child for my parents.

I had to wear a school uniform, just like all the other girls in the USSR. It was a dark brown dress with a black apron. I hated that uniform so much that every day after school, I took it off and threw it under a chair. My mom always scolded me, but I continued this personal little protest.

At school, I had bad behavior, too. My frustrated teachers called my parents to school every week. It seemed like my mom and dad had to visit my school to meet with my teachers just like they had to go to work! However, I earned very good marks. Fortunately, my parents considered getting high marks and gaining knowledge more important than everything else, so they never scolded me for my naughtiness at school. I know that they even laughed about it between themselves. During my lessons, I liked to play cards or visit with my classmates. If classes weren't interesting to me, I would read books or daydream. I often argued with my teachers. Of course they didn't like this and banished me from their classrooms. I would then go to the nearest park, walking there alone. A day of punishment turned out to be a wonderful penalty for me! Although I missed many lessons, I had the highest marks in my class.

I didn't worry too much about school. Instead, I looked forward to my fun times outdoors with all of my friends. It was so great to jump into big, big puddles after the rain and then return home like wet chickens. We played outside every day without any adults around to bother us. We climbed trees, explored abandoned lofts, and gathered on roofs of high houses. These places were our kingdoms where nobody could disturb us.

Stray dogs and cats were among our friends. We knew all of their shelters, and we were acquainted with their puppies and kittens. We enjoyed letting them feast on food which we secretly brought from home. I think that if wandering tigers or lions had come to our town, we would have made friends with them too. We played war and had little fights constantly, so we always had bruises and scars. These were our awards for our daring childhood.

When I was eight years old, life was an amazing time for care-free laughter, unbelievable secrets, and incredible adventures. Yes, I was a rebellious and stubborn little girl, but I will always remember my childhood as a happy and lighthearted time, when I thought I could do everything.

Tania Taranda, Belarus
Parkway AEL Program

Uyen Pham

I was born on August 11, 1978, in Rach Gia Province, an area in southern Vietnam famous for the abundance of rice fields and fishing. When I was a little girl, my family and I lived with my grandparents because my father, a Vietnamese soldier in the South Vietnam army who fought alongside the Americans during the Vietnam War, left for America. He came to America to avoid persecution by the new Communist Party when I was eighteen months old. After my grandparents passed away, my mother, my younger brother, and I moved to a small town to run a business.

When I was eighteen years old, I finished high school and entered Ho Chi Minh City University of Architecture in Saigon, the former capital of South Vietnam, renamed Ho Chi Minh City (HCMC). HCMC was a big city for a country girl. I got lost among the crowds of people and thousands of motorbikes and cars. I was so scared. After a few months I became more comfortable with my new life. I began to like this city because it was animated and suited for young people to learn and develop their capabilities. I lived in Saigon for five years, and then I got engaged to a Vietnamese American, now my husband. I came to America before receiving my architecture degree from HCMC University.

I met my husband through my father and my husband-to-be's uncle, Huong Nguyen, when I was in my third year of college. My father and his uncle were best friends in Seattle, Washington. At the time, Uncle Huong thought that I was only sixteen or seventeen years old and too young for marriage. However, when he found out my real age, twenty-two, Uncle Huong talked to my father about his intentions to introduce his nephew to me. Uncle Huong and my father exchanged our pictures.

In the summer of 2000, Uncle Huong's nephew called me. I was not comfortable talking with a person I knew only through a picture. However, when the conversation finished, I felt okay because my new friend was friendly. We talked on the phone for about eight months before he visited me in 2001. After that, we continued to "date" through phone conversations and e-mail. We decided on a little secret engagement when my boyfriend visited me for the second time. The third time, my fiancé and his family came to my family in Vietnam to talk about our marriage. Both our families had a large party for us in Vietnam. I came to America with my fiancé a few weeks after the engagement party.

I arrived in St. Louis in May 2002. My husband and I were married shortly thereafter in New York, where my in-laws live. We returned to St. Louis after the wedding because my husband worked and studied here. He was a part-time MBA student at Washington University (he received his degree in August 2004) while working for Wells Fargo Home Mortgage. We do not yet have children. I have studied at St. Louis Community College for the past two years. Upon completing basic college courses, I will apply to an architectural program.

My Mother

When I was one year old, and my brother was ten days old, my father left us to live in another country without connection during my childhood. My mother had to take care of us by herself. She was authoritative, hard, and not affectionate. When I was a child, I often asked myself, "Does my mother love me? Am I her birth child?" She was demanding of me, and I felt she did not love me. She forced me to do a lot of work every day. However, later I realized that her goal prepared me for my future.

My mother was beautiful. She had short black hair, smooth and silky. Her eyes were big and shined like stars in the sky. Her yellow skin was smooth like the skin of a baby. She was not tall, but her shape was daintily slender. Her face was serious. It made me afraid when I wanted to talk to her. Once, when she was talking with her friend at our home, I told her I was hungry. Her eyes stared at me, and she ordered me to kneel in my room and think about what I had done. After her friend left, she came to my room and admonished me. She never used dulcet words. She shouted loudly and beat me with her whip. Moreover, my mother forced me to do a lot of housework. She showed me how to sweep the floor, how to wash clothes and dishes, and how to cook.

My mother was my teacher in first grade. She treated me differently from the other students because I was her child. When I made a mistake, she punished me in front of my class with a double penalty. Other students just received warnings, or they had to write one page about a new word. Every time I wanted her help, I had to wait until nobody in class needed her.

She did not pay attention to my questions. I talked to her when we got home. She told me that because I was her child, she wanted my classmates to see that she was a fair teacher.

When I became a teenager, my mother trained me in her business. Her teacher income did not provide enough money for her family, so she rented a kiosk in my hometown market to sell consumer goods. She and I went to the market in early morning, and in the evening, she asked me to sell bread along the street. Sometimes I met my classmates. They mocked me. I wanted to quit, but my mother did not allow it. I did not ask why because in my mind I always thought my mother hated me. Thus, the best way was to be silent and do what she wanted. I wished that I could leave her.

At eighteen, my dream about living far from my mother came true. I passed the university exam and left home to study at an architectural school in Saigon, the big city in my country. However, Saigon was too big for a country girl. I got lost in the crowded streets. I could not figure the correct way to my dorm. Every evening, I stood in front of my dorm and remembered my hometown and every detail of my country life. I thought of my mother and what she was doing. Did she remember me? I cried when I thought about her. I began to wish I could return to my hometown rather than live in the big city. I did not dare call home because I was afraid I would cry on the phone.

I began to understand my mother when I spent the first month with my four roommates. I knew how to do housework better at college than my four friends because my mother had trained me when I was in second grade. When my friends did the housework, I saw they did it incorrectly. In school, they lagged behind me. They did not know how to manage their study time. They could not wake up on time to go to school. They did not know how to be judicious with their words and were unreasonable with the people around them. In addition, my friends were not able to manage their budgets. They always asked me for money at the end of the month. I was happy because my mother had shown me through her business how to keep a budget. I felt that I loved my mother more than forever. Every night, I thought of her and cried. I was contrite because I had misunderstood her.

After all, I realized that my mother did not hate me. She had trained me in the hardest ways because she thought of my future. I called my mother and cried like a baby. I told her I loved her and missed her. My mother also cried and told me she had never hated me. She told me she loved me very much. She said she had not shown her love to me because she was afraid she could not teach me to become a responsible person. She was glad because I understood her goal. After that, my mother and I talked to each other like friends. I shared with her my thoughts, my feelings. I did not see her serious face anymore, but instead love and tenderness. I understood the proverb, "The language of love between mother and daughter is universal."

Uyen Pham, Vietnam
Parkway AEL Program
St. Louis Community College

Dhoksi Helmi

I was born September 3, 1960, in Fier, a big city in Albania. It was considered an industrial city because petroleum was produced, and it was also a big center for agriculture because it was favored by its geographical position. I grew up in a not very big house that belonged to my parents. I had two brothers and a sister, and I was the oldest child. When I was eleven years old, my father passed away, and my mom took care of us. She was really strong and was both a father and mother to us.

In 1979, I graduated from a high school which specialized in business. In 1981, I received a certificate in business. I married and had two daughters. I worked in my profession for eleven years in a trading enterprise in several cities in Albania. We had to move often because my husband's job as a prosecutor required a lot of moving.

From 1991 until 2001, I worked as a secretary of the court of my native town. In 2001, I won the lottery to come and live in the United States, so my family and I moved to St. Louis. New experiences were ready for me here because at that time I didn't understand English at all, and I couldn't communicate. Later on I got more involved in the American lifestyle, and now I am a college student.

I am happy for my daughters' success in school. My older one attends Saint Louis University, and the younger one is a junior at Lindbergh High School.

I miss my country every day that I am away from it, but surprisingly, I missed St. Louis during the two months that I visited my country this past summer. Now I can say that Albania and St. Louis are equal to me. I like to watch TV, especially the Oprah Winfrey show, because I think

it is interesting, and I think she is a very generous woman. I also like to travel with my family to places I haven't seen before, and St. Louis is a perfect place to start from.

𝔜 𝔜 𝔜

Red Easter Eggs in a Porcelain Bowl

I was born in the small country of Albania. For more than fifty years, my country had been in a communist system. My childhood was not as it was for children somewhere else, for example, in the United States.

When I was little, I went with my grandmother to church. We practiced the Christian Orthodox religion. The church was close to my grandmother's house. It was big and beautiful. I remember everything that was inside my church. Huge chandeliers hung from the ceiling with candles instead of lamps, and they were shining. Its wall paintings were very attractive, and the saints in them looked as if they were alive. It seemed like Michelangelo had painted them. I liked to study those paintings. While I was looking at them, I created a vision about God and about the saints too. I thought God and the saints always helped people.

One day, in 1967, my grandmother explained to me that we could not go to church anymore because the government decided so. The law closed many churches in my country. The government said, "All young people should help destroy the churches." I saw the buildings coming down, as if they were made of clay. For old people, especially, this was a bad and a strange thing. They could not believe what was going on. I remember my grandmother saying, "If we help destroy those churches, God is going to punish us. Our God will not protect us anymore. The churches are saints' places." (My church was big, and the government decided it should become a cinema.)

After this, we were not supposed to celebrate Christmas anymore. All my grandmother's children and grandchildren used to celebrate Christmas together at her house. We had enjoyed those days. My grandmother said, "I don't care about the law. I make the law in my home. Our traditions will be the same. My children are going to come and see me and their father for Christmas." We continued to celebrate together but without presents for adults. Our parents gave us only games as gifts.

We used to be together for Easter too. My grandmother bought presents—clothes, shoes, or sandals—for all her grandchildren. She dyed eggs before 1967, too. Now this custom was forbidden by law, but my grandmother continued to dye eggs for many years after 1967. We kept those eggs hidden. If anybody saw us, we would be in big trouble, as we were one day.

My cousin Dhimitri was a naughty child. He took one of the dyed eggs and showed it to neighborhood children. All the children came to my grandmother's house, waiting for dyed eggs. My grandma said, "No way! I am going to give each of you an egg, but I have white eggs only. I don't know where Dhimitri found this dyed egg."

In the evening, one of the children's parents came to our house and said to my grandmother, "Have you dyed eggs for Easter? Do you know about the law?"

My grandmother answered, "What are you talking about? Ask your child. I gave him a white egg." From that day until 1990, we didn't dye eggs. We were afraid that somebody would spy and tell the police. Breaking a law in a communist regime was a horrible thing, and my grandmother had broken a law.

Now in Albania, everybody is free to practice his or her religion. People honor Christmas, dye Easter eggs, and go to church. My church turned back to a church. My grandmother died before that happened. I wanted so much that she could go back to her church. Since 1990, I have dyed eggs for Easter every year in memory of my grandmother. I fill a porcelain bowl with red eggs and give them to the children.

Dhoksi Helmi, Albania
St. Louis Community College

Chiehli Lee

My name is Chiehli Lee. I was born in a small village in Taiwan. There were six other members in my family, including my parents, two brothers, and two sisters.

I was educated for sixteen years. In 1983 I graduated from the Chinese Military Academy and served as an officer in the army of Taiwan for ten years. In my spare time, I enjoyed running, hiking, and biking because all these are fun and healthy.

Four years ago, Naomi, my daughter, was born, and I quit my job so that I could take care of her with all my heart. Last year, my wife had an opportunity to study at Saint Louis University. I not only hoped that my wife could concentrate on studying but also that we could live all together. Those are the reasons why we decided to come to St. Louis.

Our Paradise

As a child, I lived in a small village in southern Taiwan. The weather in that region was very hot. Therefore, swimming became the most popular activity around there. I would go swimming with my friends in the summer every day. There was no swimming pool in the area. (In fact, I never went to a swimming pool before I started middle school.) For this reason we usually swam in a pond where other older friends swam, too.

One day, we arrived at the pond. We took off our clothes and put them under a tree beside the water. Then we started our happy time. We played "hide and seek" in the water, we dived for the coins we had thrown in before, we competed with each other for who could keep himself in the water for the longest time. We really had an enjoyable time.

After swimming, we wanted to pick some wild fruits as usual. Then, a terrible thing happened to us. All our clothes had disappeared! We looked around the pond over and over again, but we couldn't find them. As a result of our discussion, we needed a volunteer to go for help. However, without string, we couldn't make clothes from leaves, and without clothes, no one was willing to be the volunteer! Thus, we were disappointed and started crying.

About ten minutes later, we heard a voice from the other side of the pond.

"Hi, boys. What are you doing here?"

We saw a middle-aged man who came out from behind a tree. He didn't look so angry. I stopped crying and asked him, "Excuse me, sir, do you . . ."

No sooner had I asked than he replied, "Yes, I do."

I asked again, "Would you please . . ."

The man interrupted and said, "This is a private land. You are not allowed here without permission. No wonder you have received some punishment!"

Of course, we had been punished! Afterwards, we took back our clothes. If anyone asked us, "Will you go there again someday?" our answer would be, "Why not? We'll just hide the clothes well or bring spare clothes." After all, the pond was a paradise for children in summer.

Chiehli Lee, Taiwan
International Institute

Yael Shavit-Shotland

Iwas born in the summer of 1963 in Haifa, a city in the north of Israel, by the Mediterranean Sea. I grew up in Haifa, where people from different cultures and religions lived together.

After high school, I did my military service, like everyone. I traveled for six months, like everyone, and then I was ready to go to college. I studied occupational therapy in Haifa University, and after graduation, I worked as an OT, especially with people with severe mental disorders.

I met my husband on a trip to Sinai, a beautiful desert with a very romantic beach and mountains. We climbed together to the top of Mount Sinai, where people believe Moses got the Ten Commandments from God. It was a full moon night, and I knew, "This is the one."

My husband is a biologist researcher. We came to the United States for his research, to work at Washington University in St. Louis. We have three lovely children: a ten-year-old girl, a seven-year-old boy, and a one-year-old girl. Although we enjoy our time here in St. Louis very much, we plan to go back to Israel soon.

Memory of a Four-Year-Old Girl

1967. Three weeks, and I would turn four. I had a new baby sister, two weeks old, and we had just moved to a new house in a new neighborhood. So many new beginnings. I lived in this new big house, in a

new room all to myself. (Later, I would share the room with my sister; meanwhile, she was sleeping with my mom.) My brother was four years older than I, and he had his own room, too. However, everything was confusing. We had so many things to be excited with and to be happy about. But my mom was tense and not happy at all. My dad was not with us; he had gone into the army. That meant that war was at the door.

It was a confusing time because I could see the difference between what I felt with all these beginnings and good things that were happening to my family—and the mood people had around us. I saw my mom and my neighbors worried, sad, nervous, maybe even scared.

And then, the Six Days War started. We didn't know then that it would take only six days; we did not know how it would end. We just knew that all the countries surrounding us wanted to fight and did not want us there. It happened almost forty years ago, and I remember it like it was yesterday. I remember the tension. I remember my mom listening to the radio and staring at us to be quiet. Orit, a friend of mine five years old, came over, and we were playing and talking. We did not talk loud, but I could hear my mom saying, "Now, be quiet!" and listening to the radio.

We lived in the city by the shore, so we did not hear the sounds of the war, only the alarms—alarms during the days and during the nights. And I remember the night, in the middle of the night, when the alarms started. Each of us had his duty, his or her responsibility. My chore, as a four-year-old girl, was to get up by myself, to put my slippers on, and to be ready. My brother, eight years old, had to take care of me. My mom took care of my baby sister. The night when the alarms began, I remember waking up. It was dark, and the door to my room was closed. I got up. I remember sitting on the edge of my bed, wearing my pajamas, my feet in my slippers, and waiting—waiting for my brother to come and take me. I recall the darkness, the door opening, and my big brother coming in. I was proud of myself for being ready before he came in.

We all went together down to the shelter, with our neighbors. I didn't feel any fear. I was not crying or screaming. I was excited, a four-year-old girl pleased to have done her job, to be part of the adults' world—a girl that did not understand what a war really meant, what those alarms meant—only feeling the unrest and the turmoil. I do not remember anything else from that war, just that night that I was "independent," got up by myself, and was ready even before my brother came to help me. I felt proud, and I felt good. These feelings continue with me and are carved in my memory.

Now, my ideas about war are so much different. I cannot put the words "excitement" and "good" together with "war." I can just hope that my children will not have to go through this kind of experience.

Yael Shavit-Shotland, Israel
Parkway AEL Program

Percy Mutekanga Kintu

My name is Percy Mutekanga Kintu. I was born in Swaziland. The oldest of three brothers, I grew up in a family where education was very important. My parents are both teachers. My mother teaches elementary school, and my father, high school history. Our family moved as my parents followed teaching jobs. I lived in Swaziland, Uganda, and South Africa before moving to Botswana when I was five years old. Each nation is different, and I found advantages and disadvantages in each. I am a citizen of Uganda, and I speak four African languages.

As I was growing up, I remember a remote-controlled airplane that my dad bought me. This was my favorite toy, and I decided to become a pilot one day. One of my brothers had a toy police car, and the other one a toy truck.

I attended a private school in Botswana before high school. My mother was teaching there, so part of my tuition was paid. Later, I graduated from a public high school. I studied English during my school years.

This is going to be my second year studying in the United States. So far I am enjoying my stay here, but I must say it was rough in the beginning. I really didn't know anyone at my new high school in St. Louis, and it was so hard for me to settle in. I told myself that the best thing to do was to sit with the new kids at meals so that I wouldn't feel left out. I therefore started making new friends every day, and in the end, it worked out. I was not alone anymore.

I was so surprised to see how diverse this school was. I even got to meet some other students from Africa. This was so exciting because I got to ask them a lot of questions about how they felt the first day they went to school, and how they managed to settle in.

By the end of the school year I was surprised at how many friends I had made. I was then a different person. I finished high school at the age of sixteen, and now I am a freshman in college. I plan to study a business major. I hope to go to graduate school after completing my four years in college so that I can have a very successful career.

Education, the Key to Success

Education

Education, oh education
The roots of an oak tree planted in the Okavango delta
Watered well and watched to grow
Whenever you are lost there is no hope
But whenever you are found, there is hope
You are the morning dream that sets mind at rest
Yes, education, you are the
Key to success.

I remember that time as if it were yesterday. I was eleven years old and at the peak of learning as much as I could. I always wanted a challenge, especially anything that involved education. I even had this huge rivalry with one of my friends involving who would be ranked number one in class when it came to test scores.

It was a Monday morning, and the atmosphere in the class was filled with everyone mumbling about their past weekends and all the fun activities they had done. Unlike the rest, I was paying attention to the teacher's announcements.

She told us about the last assembly of the school year, where each class had to have a representative who was going to present something in front of the whole school. At that moment everyone in the class was silent because no one wanted to be picked by the teacher to perform in front of the whole school. The teacher asked for volunteers. I was not surprised to see my rival put up his hand first. I immediately put mine up, and the teacher accepted. She then told the class that she needed two more volunteers, just for the sake of competition. No one responded. She then resorted to a long lecture, which in the end did manage to convince two more students to volunteer.

The teacher then told us that this year's seventh-grade representative was to recite a poem from our English textbook entitled "Education," and that out of the four volunteers, including me, only one would make it on stage.

We were each handed the poem and told to practice reciting it by heart every day. The performance would be on Friday, so the representative would be chosen on Thursday that very week. I was so excited that I couldn't wait to get back home and start practicing right away. For the next three days, I practiced very hard, and whenever I felt like I was falling off track, I would remind myself of what my rival would be doing at that very moment. Right after that, I would jump up and start practicing over and over again.

The moment finally arrived. It was a warm Thursday afternoon. We were told to go in turns, right in front of the class. The winner would be announced at the end of the day. I remember trembling in fear in front of my classmates; the first signs of nervousness had started to show. The first two students were okay but made some errors here and there. Then went my rival, who recited so perfectly that I became even more nervous than before.

I was up next, and I told myself to just remember what I had practiced the days before. I had no errors, and I was confident I had won. At the end of the day, the teacher congratulated all the participants for jobs well done. She also reminded us that there would have to be one winner. The name was announced, and at first I thought I was dreaming. I realized I wasn't when the teacher repeated the name: Max, my friend and my rival! I was confused and demanded right away to know why I was not chosen. The teacher said that it was because I recited the poem too fast, and that a poem was to be said slowly since it was sending out a message to the audience.

I was so sad that I didn't speak to anyone after class. That night, I sat down and read the poem to myself slowly. That's when it suddenly hit me. I read it so intensely that I actually discovered the significance behind the poem—unlike before, when I was practicing just for the sake of competition. I looked on the bright side and told myself that I was a winner in my own way, by actually getting the message of the poem. The best part of my story is that ever since then, I have never forgotten that poem. This poem has helped me a lot in many tough situations, especially through decision-making involving education, and I am glad that I did emerge as a winner.

Percy Mutekanga Kintu, Botswana
St. Louis Private High School Graduate, 2007 (at 16 years of age)

Nayna Patel

I was born in Wada, India, in 1977, where my father had a big farm. He decided to expand his business, so we moved to a nearby town, Mandvi, which was next to the Indian Ocean. We lived in a small house in the middle of Mandvi, where everything was close, from school to marketplaces. Along with my parents, I lived with my three elder sisters, Narmad, Sarswati, and Jigna, and my sweet Aunt Ganga. My mother stayed very busy after we moved to Mandvi because she had to go back to Wada on the weekends to work on the farm. This work, plus raising four girls, was a lot for one person, so my aunt helped my mom.

When I was in second grade, we moved again—to Bhuj, sixty kilometers away. This is where I continued growing up. It was a nice town and not as crowded at Mandvi. It was bigger, too. Here, everything wasn't close to our house, and we had to ride our bicycles to school. Here, too, my brother, Hardik, was born. We were very excited to have a cute baby brother to take care of.

My sisters and I loved sports, everything from cricket to track and field. In school we always got prizes and awards for various athletic competitions. Along with sports, I also loved art and enjoyed drawing and painting. In school, I was good in all the sciences, except mathematics. I just got a passing grade in math until ninth grade, when my uncle's best friend, Janti, came to stay in our house to tutor us during vacation. He was a teacher in Ahmedabad. He helped me go through the whole textbook. At last, I understood the logic of math. After that, I realized that if I put my mind to anything, I could do it. Also, Janti showed me how one teacher can make a difference in a student's life.

I earned my bachelor's degree in commerce at the University of Gujarat. After college, one of my aunt's relatives, who lived in the United States, introduced me to my future husband while he was visiting India from the United States. We spent a couple of days getting to know each other before he returned to America. I felt comfortable with him, and we arranged to be engaged. We tried a long-distance relationship, exchanging phone calls, letters, and cards. After a year of separation, he returned to India in December 1999, and we got married. Again, he had to return to the United States, and I left my country and my family to join him three months later.

It was all a strange, new world and life that I was beginning in St. Louis. I had never been outside India before. With no family to help me, I was living with my husband, someone I had only had a brief contact with in India, and who I had committed the rest of my life to. It was a rough road, with its many highs and lows–smooth pavement and rough potholes, some wrong turns in life, some right ones. However, I am very happy and grateful now to be here in St. Louis.

The Bakery

Does it happen to you that the same childhood memory stays in your mind like it just occurred yesterday? I have forgotten a lot of things over time, but I will never forget "my" bakery.

My mother often sent me there; I never turned down an opportunity to go. The bakery stood a half-mile past the large marketplace. Pedestrians, rickshaws, motorcycles, and bicycles crowded the narrow, zig-zag road. I walked by various stands and booths that sold everything from vegetables, fruits, pottery, items for home décor, stationery, and clothing to electronics. I passed a toy store and candy stores, too, but they never took away my attention from the bakery.

I always noticed the aroma coming toward me as I got closer. I imagined the rolls, cakes, pastries, and other items row after row inside glass cabinets. Fresh from the oven, they were neatly decorated in reds, whites, greens, and other pretty colors. In my mind's eye, I could see the creamy cakes in different shapes, from butterflies to cricket bats.

However, I loved the sweet rolls best. Oh! They were crunchy on the outside and creamy on the inside—the perfect combination. The crust was a thin flaky dough in many layers, and a light pink cream filling was inserted through the side. When I ate one, it just melted in my mouth. . . .

When I finally reached the bakery, a big crowd was usually there. The shop bustled with people going in and out. Old and young, but mainly mothers and young girls, stood in long lines waiting for their chance to purchase. I wasn't big enough to see inside. Many of the local customers recognized me, so someone would say, "Go, Sweetie. You can go first." I squeezed around people's legs to the front. (At that time, I was thinking it would be nice if I were a baker's daughter; that way, I could sit in the corner of the shop and munch and munch all day long.) The bakers, a couple of young gentlemen who always smiled, never asked me what I needed. They knew what I loved, so they packed the rolls for me, and I was on my way.

The smell of the bakery was then in my backpack. While I was going back home, I had to resist the temptation to eat one. I had enough rolls for everyone in my family. My brother and sisters could smell them, and they jumped excitedly towards me to get one. To see the happy, smiling faces made my wait worthwhile.

The delicious aroma from that bakery I have never found anywhere else. The memory is not just of the rolls, but also of the sights and sounds and smells of my trek to the shop. In addition, it conjures up recollections of my family at home enjoying themselves and having a good time. For most children, chocolate is a treasure, but for me, it was the sweet rolls at the Paris Bakery in Bhuj, India. My mouth waters just thinking about them.

Nayna Patel, India
Parkway AEL Program
St. Louis Community College
University of Missouri–St. Louis

Marin Markov

I was born in the small town of Montana, Bulgaria, located at the foot of Stara Planina Mountain. Montana is more famous for its past than for its present. It is an ancient city of commerce built by the Romans when Bulgaria was part of the vast Roman Empire. Even though during socialism several big plants were built in the town, it never became a typical industrialized center. In respect to interpersonal relationships, the town continued to live in its small patriarchal world, in which everyone was part of someone else's life, and the whole community was like one big family. In the atmosphere of this town I formed my understanding of good, evil, dignity, and success, and my whole spiritual world was shaped.

My parents convinced me that a career as an officer in the Bulgarian army was a good professional choice for me, and after I finished high school, I went to a school for military engineers. Quickly after I started my actual work in the army, however, I realized that the rudeness and the strange understanding of humanity spread among the commanders were incompatible with my values in life. Leaving the army was the only choice I had if I wanted to avoid a major psychological breakdown. I became jobless at a period of very high unemployment in Bulgaria. At this time I was married, with a little child to be responsible for. Finding a job was not simply a desire; it was a painfully obvious necessity. There was no one willing to hire me so I had to hire myself. I started my own business. Persistence and hard work were the keys to my business success. The company was profitable, and I was able to hire five people to work for me.

When my sister-in-law headed for America, I started considering the possibility of following her steps. Her words that America is open for hardworking people with initiative sounded like a promise for success. When I also won a green card, I moved with my family to St. Louis, leaving the business in my father-in-law's hands. Curiosity to see new places and new people, the thrill of the challenge, and my interest to understand what makes America respected in the world were the major motives for my arrival.

Bulgarians have an old saying that the stone is heavy in its own place, meaning that a person is most successful where his or her roots are. After almost five years living in America, I am not sure I can fully agree with this, nor yet can I fully reject it.

The Railway Line

Everybody has unforgettable moments in his life. I want to write about one such moment in my childhood. I was born and grew up in a small town in Bulgaria. The town is called Montana. The name of this town dates as far back as 950 years ago. Montana has a lot of historical landmarks. These old sites were not exciting for me and my friends. We children had our secret places to play, and they were more appealing than the historical places in the town. One of these places was the freight train station.

On one windy day, I, a seven-year-old boy, and my friends Ivo and Zari decided to go there. We knew from boys bigger than us that if we put nails on the rails, the passing train would turn them into flat metal sticks. Captivated in discussion of what direction to put the nails, we forgot we were sitting between the tracks, unaware of the danger of a coming train.

I was the one that first saw the train. The huge machine was moving noiselessly toward us. To my surprise, I was unable to react. I was numb.

My fingers and legs did not listen to me. The train was getting closer. I looked down at my helpless feet on the dirty, oily stones. I looked up at the gloomy sky and thought I saw the end of my life. When I looked down again, there was no train anymore. I saw the three-headed dragon from my storybook flying against me. It was so close that I even heard the uniform chattering of its teeth! The monster suddenly roared. The sound was deafening—a cry of grinding metal.

Suddenly everything became very quiet around me. I closed my eyes, ready to fly away with the dragon. The wind was blowing strongly at me, as if making the last attempt to help me. I was like a rooted one-hundred-year-old tree. Even the strongest storm would have been unable to shake me. All at once, someone pushed me strongly. I turned over the rails and dropped onto the ground. The air flow of the passing train was hitting my face. The clatter of its wheels was unbearable. The earth was shaking. My heart was beating with the same rhythm—tap, tap, tap. The moment seemed to last an eternity. The train stopped not far away from us, and I heard the angry shouting of the men that got off it. I looked at my friends. We got up quickly onto our feet and ran away.

My story remained a secret kept between me and my friends. We never said anything about it to our parents. We were afraid that they would punish us. The boy that had saved my life was Zari. Now, when I remember this story, I want to tell him, "Thank you. Thank you, Zari, for helping me to get on the train of Life."

This train has a lot of stations. New people get on. Others like my beloved grandparents, get off and become part of the past. I met my wife at one of the railway stations, and it was the beginning of something new—our marriage, and the life of our son. Without Zari's help, I wouldn't be able to enjoy the journey.

Marin Markov, Bulgaria
St. Louis Community College

Kun "Mary" Wang

I was born in May 1972. The city, Xian, where I grew up, is a magnificent city in northwest China with a long history. I spent my childhood with my family in that area until 1982.

Then we moved to Jiangou Province, Yangtze River delta. A few years later, I graduated from high school. After that, I attended Nanjing University with a major in history. Meanwhile, my elder sister joined the army, and now she is a public prosecutor. I love her, and she is my good example.

After my graduation from the university, I worked in an import/export business. Later, I ran an advertising company for several years. The last job I held before I came to the United States was in a real estate company as marketing director. Over ten years of work experience made me have an interest in public relations and communications. I have a dream that one day I will go to the university to further my education in these areas.

I came to St. Louis for love. My husband had been waiting for me so long, and he was looking forward to enjoying life with me. I like travel and sports. Every year I arrange a long-distance trip, such as to Tibet or Thailand. And every week I spend a lot of time on sports, such as badminton, tennis, and swimming. Life is a long road. I'm a busy, happy traveler.

The Outdoor Movies

About twenty-five years ago, when I was a little child, I lived with my parents in Xian City, in northwest China. At that time, my parents worked in an institute doing research. The time was wonderful, and it always crashes into my mind, especially the memory of watching the Sunday outdoor movies.

During the week, all the children of people who worked at the institute were praying for good weather on Sunday and were looking forward to the special event of the day. When Sunday came, although the movie would be played in the evening, we kids went again and again from noontime on to see if there was equipment on the playground. If there was, we would rush into our homes yelling with excitement. Our parents knew what would happen. Movie plans were on! They would prepare for dinner, and we could sense their happiness for us.

At about 4 o'clock, we children took the chairs and benches from our houses and put them on the playground, row by row. We played games, jumped from here to there, talked and laughed with each other. One and a half hours later, we all went home for dinner.

After dinner, it turned dark while parents and children walked to the playground. Before the movie started, it was a good opportunity for people to chat with each other. Usually at 7:30, the movie began. We children didn't care about the story or the roles in the movie. We just liked to enjoy the moment—and that feeling of waiting.

Kun "Mary" Wang, China
Parkway AEL Program

Lela Jasarevic

I was born February 10, 1966, in Ivangrad, Montenegro. When I was three months old, I left Montenegro and went with my parents to live in Sarajevo, Bosnia. (At that time Bosnia, Montenegro, Croatia, Slovenia, Macedonia, Serbia, and two provinces, Kosovo and Vojvodina, were one country named Yugoslavia.)

Four years later, my father died. I was four years old, and my brother was four months old. My mother took good care of us, and we had everything, except a father. I grew up in Sarajevo, the capital city of Bosnia and Herzegovina, the city of my youth and love. I had my first step, my education (elementary school, high school, college), my first love, my marriage, and my first child there.

In 1992, war started in my country, and I had to leave my hometown with my two-year-old son. I left everything there: my mom, brother, husband, house, car, job, and friends. I just took my son and two suitcases and went to Austria, where my life became uncertain. In Austria I lived with my son for ten months. After ten months, my husband came to be with us. From Austria we went to Germany where something incredible happened. My second son was born. In Germany, we lived for three and a half years. Then we came to the United States.

Today we are here in St. Louis, American citizens. I am a mother, wife, full-time employee, and student again. I am happy with my family. I realize that my travels started when I was three months old, and God only knows what is going to happen tomorrow. I can pray and hope that I am done with my travels. I have found peace in this beautiful country.

The Fishing Boat

Every year my mother and brother and I went to the Adriatic Sea on vacation. We stayed in the same hotel. The people who worked in the hotel were nice to me, and I liked them a lot. I remember a day in the summer when I was six years old.

It was a perfect day. The sun blazed a hot, golden yellow, and the sky was cloudless. My mother had told me never to swim far from shore. She said that was dangerous for me. I told her not to worry. I loved to swim, and that day, I looked for my friend, Emina, who I had met there. She was the same age as me. Emina's father was a captain in the army, and she and her family had moved by the sea when Emina was one year old. We swam and swam. I forgot what my mother had told me. When we turned towards shore, people looked little, like ants. My friend was in a panic, and I was afraid too.

Just then, I saw a fishing boat coming toward us. It was red and blue, small and very old. When I told Emina, she became calm. The fisherman was an old man with a pipe in his right hand. His hair and beard were white. His skin was a golden brown from the sun, and his eyes were as blue as the Adriatic Sea. Barefoot, he wore a blue and white short-sleeved shirt and blue pants. I especially remember his face. Something in his eyes reminded me of my grandfather. When he pulled us into the boat, I felt safe and secure. I was also a little scared, but his smile encouraged me. He spoke softly to us as he brought us to the shore.

My mother was furious. She hissed at me. I was so ashamed. I wanted to tell her how I felt, but she didn't want to listen to me. I had a bad presentiment. I was in big trouble. My mother punished me. I could not eat ice cream, candy, or chocolate for one week. One week without ice cream and candy was for me a long time. But I had to accept the punishment. I promised her that I would never do something like that again. She kissed me and gave me a hug.

Everybody in the hotel knew how much I loved chocolate and ice cream. They decided to help me, and they sneaked me a little ice cream after lunch. We stayed one more week. My mom forgave me for disobeying her, and we enjoyed the rest of our vacation.

Lela Jasarevic, Bosnia
St. Louis Community College

Felix Ngassi

I was born in Makoua, R. Congo (Brazzaville) in May 1961. From 1969 to 1984, I finished, respectively, elementary, middle, and high schools.

In September 1984, upon graduation from Salvador Allende High School in Makoua, I went to study at a university in Russia. After one year of learning the Russian language in Krasnodar, Russia, I was transferred to the Russian Academy of Agriculture in Moscow, where I studied applied chemistry in agriculture for five years. I graduated in June 1990.

In addition, I continued my studies in soil science for four years for a Ph.D. in agriculture. From February 1994 to February 1996, I worked as a microbiology lab assistant at the academy. Then, from February 1996 to February 2002 I taught soil science at the Institute of Soils under V. V. Dockutsev in Moscow.

My family and I emigrated from Moscow to St. Louis in November 2002. I am married and have three sons.

The Family Trip . . . Without Me

When I was very young, I always wanted to go everywhere my parents went. The summer when I was five years old, my parents, my older brothers, and I left our village to go to a camp next to a river. The fishing was excellent there. One day my parents left for an all-day trip.

Usually for this kind of trip, people only took older children with them. The younger children, like me, were not allowed to go. However, for me that was unacceptable. I did not want to stay in the camp. When the boat left the camp without me, I started crying. In order to join the trip, someone told me that I should run along the river, following the boat. I decided to follow my parents. I hoped my parents would see me and pick me up. I ran probably about a mile, but they didn't see me.

The most difficult problem I faced after this was that I couldn't find my way back to the camp. I was still crying, and it was for a long time. Since I had cried so much, I got tired, and I fell asleep in the jungle. I stayed alone in the jungle for many hours.

In the evening, my parents couldn't find me once they returned to the camp. Nobody knew where I was. Thus, my parents decided to look for me in the jungle. According to their words, they found me—next to a big boa constrictor that did not allow them to come close. Finally, my father shot the snake and killed it. Then my parents took me back to the camp. Days later, they told me about the boa. I was very scared.

After all, I remember two things about this story: first, I was always taken on trips by my parents after my adventure in the jungle; and second, I learned to listen to my parents and not to go to the jungle by myself. This experience helped me to be more careful and to think a little bit before doing some things.

Felix Ngassi, Congo
International Institute
St. Louis Community College

Zhong Ling

Zhong Ling in Guangzhou

Boarding school five and a half days a week
I hated it so much.

My parents worked on Saturday
While I stayed home
  with the maids.

One was so old
  she had three gold teeth
She buried my parrot on her farm
and took me to market
  on the back of her trike cart.

Zhong Ling "Beverly Jones," China
Fifth Grade, Parkway Elementary School

Henrietta Anokhina

I was born in Leningrad (now St. Petersburg) in Russia. World War II changed our lives absolutely. I remember bombings every day and the necessity to go downstairs to have a shelter. The starving time began very soon, and every minute I felt hungry. My mother helped my sister and me to survive by sharing her small portion of bread with us. Leningrad was under siege, and the limited apportionments of bread became less and less (about 100 grams a day). My mother was a pediatrician, and she was sent to convoy sick children from the blockaded city to safety; she could take us along. It was a real rescue every time.

When the siege was finished, we returned to my native city. Postwar life was very hard too: limited food, reconstruction of destroyed buildings, bad transportation. I was involved in science, physics, and mathematics when I reached thirteen years old. I wished to get an education in experimental physics at a university, but I couldn't do it because of the strong discrimination toward Jewish people at that time.

Later, I graduated from the University of Electro-Engineering and began to work as an engineer in the Institute of Navigation. When I studied at the university, my future husband was my classmate. After graduation we fell in love and got married. Our son was born one and a half years later, and we were happy. I had my favorite husband and my favorite son and my favorite job. My life was full. I was working in the institute with interesting and brilliant people, and I felt happy.

My son's family moved to the United States in 1993. My husband and I followed them in 1996. After that I began another life, difficult but interesting too.

Fresh Bread, Ice-Cold Milk

My childhood memories go back to the hard-starving wartime. When we were evacuated during the Leningrad blockage, my mother, sister, and I happened to be in a village where we saw fresh bread and frosted milk.

It was my first impression after a long time of starving, and I remember the smell of the big round freshly baked loaf of homemade rye bread as the best fragrance in my short life. I received a big wedge of this wonderful bread. The size of the wedge taken by me seemed absolutely exciting. After endless hungry days, when we had only a strictly limited portion of bread a day (150 grams), it was a miracle. My mother, a doctor, divided the wedge of bread in three portions and warned us to eat only small pieces until we got used to eating normal food.

Beside this bread I saw a bowl with something solid and white in it. I perceived the fresh and sharp smell, and I didn't understand what it was. My mother put this bowl in warm water, kept it there several minutes, and then turned the bowl over. It was frosted milk. My sister and I cut this milk and sucked. I was an urban girl and didn't know that peasants kept milk frozen in bowls during wintertime.

Fresh bread, ice-cold milk . . . the smell of these will stay in my memory forever.

Henrietta Anokhina, Russia
Parkway AEL Program

Meejoo Flasphaler

My name is Meejoo Flasphaler, and I am from Korea. I was a secretary at a computer company for about five years. While I worked there, we had a lot of business with the United States and with Japan. I had to learn to speak both languages. I went to language school in Korea to study English and Japanese, and I found out that I had more interest in English. So I decided to travel to the United States to study more English. I graduated from the Air Academy to prepare for my career. I worked with United Airlines and later, for a travel agency.

Now, I have an American husband who is a lieutenant commander in the navy. We have a baby girl, Mina. I am enjoying staying home and taking care of my family. When I look back at myself, I am so glad that I did what I did.

The Milk Cart

I don't like winter, especially in the morning, because I had a very cold winter in my childhood. I was between fourth grade and fifth grade in Korea when we had an oil crisis. My father owned a medicine factory. During that time, he lost a lot of money. He couldn't pay bills. Finally, he had to declare bankruptcy. He decided to run away for a while, and my mom agreed.

I didn't know what was going on. But we had to move into a two-bedroom apartment in the suburbs of Seoul. I had to transfer to another

school. It was so hard for me, especially because I had a good friend. I didn't want to just let go. We stayed in our little apartment, which was okay. My father couldn't live with us; he was afraid somebody would come after him.

My mom had to go out and earn some money, but all her life after high school, she had stayed home and taken care of her family. She didn't know what she could do. Somehow she decided to deliver milk; in the Korean system, we delivered milk door to door every morning. When she started, it was late summer, and she told me it wasn't that difficult. But when winter started, my mom had to wear a heavy jacket, hat, gloves, and boots. It was so hard to pull the milk cart. Especially on snowy days, she needed somebody to help her push her cart up the hill. I found out how hard it was.

Right after I started my winter vacation, I went out with my mom. I woke up early in the morning, about 3:30 a.m. Outside it was still dark, cold, and windy. I didn't like that cold air; I didn't even want to move. When the cold air hit my face, I didn't know what to do. But I always gave a big smile to my mom, and I told her, "I like to go out with you." We talked a lot while delivering milk. I helped her all my winter vacation.

Even though my family went through a hard time because of the bankruptcy, the experience taught us what family is all about. My father started a new business, and after that we moved back to Seoul. My mom, who had worked about a year and a half, again stayed home to take care of us. During that time, I loved my family more, and I got closer to them than before. My life has changed a lot since then, but two things remain the same: my affection for my family, and my dislike of cold mornings.

Meejoo Flasphaler, Korea
Parkway AEL Program

Alejandra Keren Nixon

I was born in November of 1981 in Buenos Aires, Argentina. My beautiful family includes my three sisters, Erica, 26, Vanina, 21, and Alexia, 15.

My father, a missionary minister, was asked to come to St. Louis to be the pastor of the Hispanic church here. Vanina, Alexia, and I finished high school in the United States. Actually, I had graduated from high school in Argentina, but I decided to go to school again to learn English. Then, I started working at Missouri Baptist Medical Center as a nurse assistant. After working at the hospital for two years, I decided to go back to school. St. Louis Community College offered a writing class. I have always loved to write, so I took this class to improve my writing skills.

I met my husband, Garrett, in the United States. We met in church, and it was love at first sight. He shared his interest in learning Spanish, so I invited him to the Hispanic church. Currently, my husband and I are both members there. I am still working at Missouri Baptist Hospital, but only a few times a month.

My oldest sister is married, Vanina is working for a very good company, and my little sister is still in school. I am glad to have my whole family here in St. Louis. I have been very blessed.

The Raggedy Stranger

It all started as any other school morning, except this particular day would be different. My sisters and I were going to walk to school on our own for the first time. We had wanted to be more grown-up, and here was our opportunity! Erica was in seventh grade, I was in fourth grade, and Vanina was in second grade. Filled with excitement, we rushed out the door after breakfast.

We found ourselves alone. Although the idea of independence had seemed glorious to me, as we walked along, a weird feeling of fear came over me. I remembered all the stories that my uncle and cousins had told us about little children being hurt by strangers—or, even worse, kidnapped. However, we arrived at school without any problem, other than that Erica thought she could tell Vanina and me what to do all the way!

Later, after the final bell, I started out of the building. A large crowd of faces filled the hallway, and I quickly found myself lost among an almost cattle-like stampede of fellow students. In the chaos of searching for my sisters, I heard my name being called. I did not recognize the man's voice. While I was looking to see who was calling me, suddenly in front of me stood an old, raggedy-dressed stranger. However, he had a kind face. My sisters joined me. The man knew their names, too. The man told us that he had been sent to pick us up by our mother. "Everything will be okay," he added. We listened to the man and trustingly got into his truck. He kept assuring us that our mom had sent him. Once inside the truck, however, he acted very nervous. Putting the truck into gear, he started up, hoping to get away fast.

To our amazement, our mom stepped in front of the truck and started yelling at the man. We then realized we were in danger. I began to cry. My sisters screamed for help and quickly attracted the attention of other parents and classmates in the parking area. Like teamwork, the adults stopped the truck and called the police, who came and arrested the man.

Once with our mom, my sisters and I felt safe again. She hugged us and calmed us while the police asked questions. That night, after the whole scary episode, my body still shaking, I asked my mom to spend the night in my bed. We fell asleep together, holding hands.

My sisters and I had been victims of a bad dream that turned into reality—an attempted kidnapping. Our mother promised that she would never allow us to go to school by ourselves again. Our father explained to us that he and our mother would never send someone to pick us up after school. We soon learned that the man ended up in jail and had a past record of kidnapping. The police told our mom that we had been very lucky that morning, and that we should not be afraid anymore because the man would be in jail for years. It took many days for us to settle down after this event. We had a lesson on what it is to be independent. In the midst of our longing to be on our own—to be grown up!—we found out that freedom can be scary.

Alejandra Keren Nixon, Argentina
St. Louis Community College

157

Mohammad Haque

I am Mohammad S. Haque, born in Comilla, Bangladesh, in July 1954. I was the third son of my parents. I took my schooling at the Meah Bazar L.N. High School and at the Victoria Government College in Comilla, Bangladesh.

After this, I joined the war of liberation of Bangladesh and contributed to the freeing of my country. In May 1975, I became a commissioned officer of the Bangladesh army and continued my service until I retired as a major. I had a very successful work record in the army in different command and staff appointments. In addition, I worked in the United Nations Iraq-Kuwait Observation Mission (UNIKOM) for one year, 1995–1996.

During my service in the army, I earned a bachelor of liberal arts and a master's degree in political science from the National University in Dhaka, Bangladesh. After my retirement from the army in February 2003, I worked in a garments export industry as a general manager of production.

In June 2004, my immigrant visa, along with those of my wife and son, were processed and confirmed through the local American Embassy in Dhaka. My wife, son, and I decided to come to the United States on November 27, 2004, with the ultimate aim of settling down here. My son Shahed is a student at Saint Louis University.

Since January 2005, my wife and I have been attending English-language classes at the International Institute in St. Louis to improve our English skills. We are eager to master the colloquial expressions and the American accent.

My Childhood Memory

My childhood memory that I remember most is an incident of being away from my home without notifying my parents. This made them worried and nervous. I was at the age of six.

One fine morning, my mother gave me some money and asked me to buy some sweets from a shop, as we had been expecting some guests on that day. After going to the shop in the market, I met some of my friends and came to know that our school team would play a friendly football match with a neighboring school team. Our team would be leaving within a short time. Hearing this—and without thinking about the consequences—I joined my friends to see the game. The whole day I spent with my friends, watching the game and enjoying the time. In the evening, instead of returning home, I went to a friend's house where I stayed overnight. It was all so amazing and interesting I even forgot to get a message to my parents about my whereabouts.

Surprisingly, in the morning when I woke up, I noticed that my friend's father while going through the newspaper, had found my name and address, including my recent photograph. The article in short said, "The boy in the picture has been missing from his home since yesterday. He might have been kidnapped." Seeing this, I was astonished and got nervous. Without any delay my friend and his father took me to my home. On the way home, my friend asked me about this episode, and I narrated the whole story. Hearing this, my friend's father advised me that at my age, I should not leave my home without prior permission from my parents.

On my coming back home, my parents got relief from a very traumatic episode. Although my mother initially got angry, my father consoled her, saying I was back home safe! My father thanked my friend's father, who had brought me home.

When I look back on my childhood years, out of a series of memories, this particular incident appears to me first. It makes me laugh, and it makes me think, "How could I have done such a foolish thing?" However, the lesson I learned from that time was that one should feel obligated to leave some message to his parents prior to leaving home!

Mohammad Haque, Bangladesh
International Institute

Dania Urbina-Loaiza

Iwas born on April 11, 1962, in a small town named Acolman, close to Mexico City. I am the oldest of six children; two of my siblings passed away when they were babies. I have two brothers, Luis and Juan, and one sister named Sagrario, who I am very close to.

I attended a Catholic elementary and middle school. I couldn't go to high school because my parents didn't have the money to send me to a private school anymore. Public schools were out of the question because they were not considered to be places for good education. Since I had three siblings in private school, my parents thought it would be better for me to study to become a secretary. They wanted me to start working and help support the family.

I attended secretarial school for four years and then began working at the age of eighteen as a secretary for a Japanese company. One year later, I moved to an American company that allowed me to continue studying. I began high school when I was nineteen years old. After that I went to the university, which was one of my dreams. During that time I had some promotions at work. When I was twenty-seven years old, I finished my studies at the university as a public accountant. By that time I was the manager of the logistics department.

After graduation, I married Edgar Loaiza, whom I had dated for quite a long time. We lived in Mexico City for two years. My daughter, Dania Eunice Loaiza, was born there when I was thirty years old. Three years later we moved to Saltillo, a town in northern Mexico, because of my husband's work. My son, Octavio, was born there in 1996.

Two years later we moved again, this time to the United States. My husband was working for an American company, DaimlerChrysler, and he was moved to St. Louis. It was a great opportunity for him. He was sent here only for two years, but so far we have been here for six years. At first, the change was a bit challenging for all of us. Language was one of the first barriers, but we all have been doing our best. Recently the company decided that they want him to work here instead of Mexico. The decision was hard to make, but we think it is the best one for our family, so we will stay. My heart, however, is still in Mexico where the rest of my family lives. It is important to mention that we have been so fortunate to count on the good friends we have made in America.

The Broken Broom

Our family reunions take place in a small town called Acolman, close to Mexico City. Here, we still have a peaceful time, without the noise of the big city. My parents, my two brothers, my sister, and I reminisce back to our adolescent life in the house where we grew up.

The last time we were gathered back in our old home, my brothers, Luis and Juan, shared one of my most embarrassing yet comedic stories that happened to me at the age of seventeen. It all started one rainy day when I was done mopping our white ceramic floor, which my mom always insisted on being spotlessly clean. (I had to do most of the cleaning in our house, not only because I was the oldest, but also because cleaning was considered a woman's chore.) I felt like I had worked hard that day, and the tile floor looked really nice, at least to me. Suddenly, my two younger brothers, who by that time were taller than me, entered with their muddy shoes.

That specific day, I had lots of homework, and I was not in the mood to tolerate their laziness. I screamed at them, "Take off your shoes!" They did not bother to listen and started to laugh at my frustration. That was it. . . .

I took the nearest cleaning tool, which turned out to be a broom, and began chasing them like a maniac. I finally reached the younger of my brothers, Juan, who was still laughing, and swung the broom with all my might. As I chased my other brother, I realized I was holding only the remains of what used to be the broom. I still remember Juan's face; he was astonished! He couldn't believe what had just happened.

I felt so bad that I wanted to hug him, but I realized he was not ready for that. As crazy as it sounds, the only thing I said was, "Take off your shoes next time." Later on, you can imagine the trouble I was in with my parents because of my lack of self-control. My mom was mad at me for several days; my dad understood better. Actually, he could never be mad at me for very long.

When we talked about this particular event, my whole family went into uncontrollable laughter. "I was lucky the broom got broken!" said my brother Luis. My family, especially my daughter, was amazed that I could have ever done such a horrible thing. For most of my life, I have kept this memory a secret, afraid that someone might find out what I did. My lovely brothers revealed it, and I couldn't do anything but laugh. Of course, I still feel embarrassed.

Dania Urbina-Loaiza, Mexico
Parkway AEL Program

꒦ ꒦ ꒦

Our Reunions

We all have memories. Some are good, and some are bad. The happiest memories I have occurred when I have visited my grandparents in Mexico.

Every two years my mom's family tries to get together at my grandparents' house. There, we eat and spend some quality time together. My grandparents' home is not exactly the richest and biggest house, but that never stops my cousins and me from having fun.

Outside the house, we climb a large tree full of *higos,* or figs. Once ripe, this juicy fruit is pink in the middle and black on the outside. We eat so many higos, we feel like we will burst. I can even still picture the juicy nectar dripping down our chins.

Afterwards, we eat tender lamb with tacos and lots of spicy salsa. But what really lights up the evening are the comic stories of my mom and her brothers and sister. One story that still embarrasses my mom tells of how my mother furiously broke a broom on my uncle's back during an adolescent fight. I was surprised that my gentle mother would do such a thing (well, not really . . . but shhh!—don't tell my mom!).

I will always cherish these memories from my childhood as I move into adulthood. I especially want to thank my grandparents for providing me with warm memories that will always be a part of me no matter where I go or who I become.

Dania Eunice Loaiza, age 12
Rockwood Middle School

Ming-Wan Huang

I was born on July 30, 1978, in a small town in Taiwan, a traditional place. Until I was fifteen years old, my parents, older sister, younger brother, and I lived with my grandparents in an old house with a big yard. The environment I grew up in is important to me because I was molded into the "me" of today in this traditional family. My personality was deeply affected by my family, both my good and bad sides.

Before I came to the United States, I was a teacher in an elementary school in Taiwan. But I felt this life was not what I wanted to live. I wanted to change my life and let it become better. Four months ago, I left my family, even though I knew I would have to face and overcome all kinds of difficulties. I came to St. Louis in order to turn over a new leaf. I am studying at Fontbonne University.

Firelight in the Fog

The clock is ticking away the seconds. My childhood seems far away from me, as if it is covered with thick fog. I cannot recall anything unless I push this fog aside purposely.

My happiness or sorrow of my whole childhood started and extended from a house. The old house in which I lived for fifteen years was built by my grandpa in person. My grandparents were serious and traditional people. Most children, including me, feared my grandpa. I remember once when my mom ladled out a bowl of mung bean sweet soup for me.

When I was relishing the soup, I glanced at Grandpa walking into the kitchen. Thus I hid myself under the table rapidly in order to avoid being seen by him. If now you ask me why I did this, I doubt I could answer you completely.

My grandparents thought that a daughter-in-law was not a true family member; they just regarded my mom as a woman who married their son, so they never treated her sincerely. Even so, day after day, my mom still had to do all chores. At that time, most household electrical appliances were not popular, except for rich people. So all housework was done by my mom's hands, including burning firewood for multiple hot baths.

The stove was located in an alley between our old house and our neighbor's. This alley, hiding a small horde of mosquitoes, was black as night all the time. Yet my mom had to stay there for an hour or two every day. I never went there without my mom. I knew roughly when she would probably be there during the day, so I usually stood at the exit of the alley and looked down into it. If my mom was there, I ran and squatted down by her side. We both looked at the firelight—chatting together. Sometimes my older sister joined us too. At that time, I always felt that our hearts hugged each other. I remember deeply that once my mom told me, "I like staying here to avoid people, even if it is dirty and dark." Although I didn't realize the inner meaning of those words at my age, I replied in my mind, "I like squatting here, even if it is dirty and dark, because you are here."

That was my childhood. As described above, I didn't live a wonderful life, but I know I have the memory of firelight to take care of me when I lose my way, when I feel scared, or even when I fall into darkness, no matter in childhood or now.

Ming-Wan Huang, Taiwan
Fontbonne University

Uyanga Tsolmonkhuu

White Moon

Today is the start of White Moon Festival! I'm so happy that I could do a back flip! Why? Because I will go to visit my grandparents, my cousins, and my friends, and I will get presents or money at each house! Sometimes we get clothes, or wallets, or candy. Candy is my favorite. One time I ate a whole box in one day!

When we go to visit, everyone has to kiss us on the cheek. When my aunt kisses my cheek, she likes to bite a little bit. Then I run away! I like to listen to my grandfather tell stories about when I was little. He likes to tell jokes, too. He has a short white beard and white and gray hair. Sometimes he doesn't move very well and has to stay in bed. I like to go to my mom's dad's house. When I say, "Hey, grandfather, get me," he grabs me and rubs his tickly beard on my chin and I laugh! We call grandfather Buraa aav. Grandmother is Buraa eej.

I have been helping my mom cook buuz for days and days. It is kind of like a flour dumpling with meat and onions inside. It is more delicious than anything! The next best thing I like is a dessert with raisins and rice. We get to eat this at every house. We go in the morning and we come back at midnight. Everyone plays Mongolian music, and some people dance. Kids go outside and play even when it's very cold and snowy. We play games and run around. Our whole family comes back very tired, but we still want to open our presents. This is our best holiday!

Uyanga Tsolmonkhuu, Mongolia
Fourth Grade, Parkway Elementary School

Acknowledgments

Eight essays were gathered for this publication with the assistance of the International Institute of St. Louis. Other resources include: Fontbonne University, Parkway Area AEL Program, Parkway School District, Rockwood School District, St. Louis Community College, The Principia School, Washington University in St. Louis, and Webster University.

We wish to thank the following ESL instructors for contributing stories from their classrooms: Elizabeth Bayer, Dianna Davis, Diane Elstner, Marjorie Hamlin, Sevil Kyazimova, Lois LeBloch, Jane Miller, Mark Slack, and Yelena Vardzigulova. The remaining stories came from Janet Morey's and Gail Schafers's students.

Our sincere gratitude goes to Allen Arpadi, our friend and photography mentor, as well as to Allied Photocolor of St. Louis. We appreciate, too, the grace, support, and professionalism expressed by everyone we have met at the Missouri Historical Society.

Special appreciation is extended to the William R. Orthwein, Jr., and Laura Rand Orthwein Foundation for its significant support in the early development of this collection of stories.